ANNO QUADRAGESIMO PRIMO

GEORGII III. REGIS.

****

C A P. XV.

An Act for taking an Account of the Population of *Great Britain*, and of the Increase or Diminution thereof. [31ſt *December* 1800.]

WHEREAS it is expedient to take an Account of the total Number of Perſons within the Kingdom of *Great Britain*, together with the progreſſive Increaſe or Diminution thereof; may it therefore pleaſe Your Majeſty that it may be enacted; and be it enacted by the King's moſt Excellent Majeſty, by and with the Advice and Conſent of the Lords Spiritual and Temporal, and Commons, in this preſent Parliament aſſembled, and by the Authority of the ſame, That within that Part of *Great Britain* called *England*, the reſpective Overſeers of the Poor, or in Default thereof, ſome ſubſtantial Houſeholder of every Pariſh, Townſhip, and Place, and within that Part of *Great Britain* called *Scotland*, ſuch Perſons as ſhall be for that Purpoſe appointed by the Sheriff Deputes, Stewart Deputes, and Juſtices of the Peace, to act in and for every Pariſh, ſhall, at the Time and in the Manner herein-after directed, ſeverally take an Account of the Number of Perſons who ſhall be actually found at the Time of taking ſuch Accounts to be within the Limits of ſuch Pariſhes, Townſhips, and Places reſpectively, and ſhall ſet down the ſeveral Particulars reſpecting the ſame, according to the Form preſcribed in the Schedule annexed to this Act.

Preamble.

The Overſeers of the Poor (or in Default thereof, ſome ſubſtantial Houſeholder) of every Pariſh and Place in England, and ſuch Perſons as ſhall be appointed by the Sheriff Deputes, Stewart Deputes, and Juſtices in Scotland, ſhall take an Account of the

Number of Perſons found within each Pariſh and Place, and ſet down the Particulars, according to the Form in the annexed Schedule.

I i

II. And

Dr William Farr, compiler of abstracts and superintendent of statistics at the General Register Office, 1838–1880: the main administrative and intellectual force behind the mid-nineteenth century censuses, (reproduced by permission of The Mansell Collection Ltd).

Public Record Office Handbooks
No 23

Making Sense of the Census

The Manuscript Returns for England and Wales, 1801–1901

Edward Higgs

London: Her Majesty's Stationery Office

© Crown copyright 1989
First published 1989
Second impression 1989
ISBN 0 11 440219 1

British Library Cataloguing in Publication Data

A CIP catalogue record for this book is
available from the British Library

HMSO BOOKS

HMSO publications are available from:

HMSO Publications Centre
(Mail and telephone orders only)
PO Box 276, London, SW8 5DT
Telephone orders 01-873 9090
General enquiries 01-873 0011
(queuing system in operation for both numbers)

HMSO Bookshops
49 High Holborn, London, WC1V 6HB   01-873 9090
(Counter service only)
258 Broad Street, Birmingham, B1 2HE   021-643 3740
Southey House, 33 Wine Street, Bristol, BS1 2BQ
(0272) 264306
9-21 Princess Street, Manchester, M60 8AS
061-834 7201
80 Chichester Street, Belfast, BT1 4JY   (0232) 238451
71 Lothian Road, Edinburgh, EH3 9AZ   031-228 4181

HMSO's Accredited Agents
(see Yellow Pages)

and through good booksellers

Printed in the United Kingdom for Her Majesty's Stationery Office.
Dd. 291109. 9/89. C15.

Contents

Preface

In the course of compiling this guide to the nineteenth-century census returns the author has received guidance and encouragement from many quarters. The following were kind enough to read preliminary drafts and make helpful comments: Mr Mark Bell and his colleagues at the Genealogical Society of Utah; Mrs Susan Lumas and Dr John Post of the Public Record Office; Mrs Pauline Saul and Lt Col I S Swinnerton of the Federation of Family History Societies; Mr Kevin Schurer of the Cambridge Group for the History of Population and Social Structure; Dr Christopher Watts of the Society of Genealogists; and Mrs Alice Woods and her colleagues at the Office of Population Censuses and Surveys. This has helped to remove errors and ambiguities from the text: those that remain are, of course, the responsibility of the author.

Mr Paul Laxton of the University of Liverpool commented on the chapters relating to the pre–1841 census returns. Mrs Jean Robin of the Cambridge Group was kind enough to supply the author with the unpublished results of her analysis of census ages and birthplaces in mid-nineteenth-century Colyton. Dr W T R Pryce of the Open University supplied invaluable information on the administration of the census in nineteenth-century Wales.

The author would also like to thank the Office of Population Censuses and Surveys for supplying him with a copy of the first five pages of a 1901 enumeration book. These contain printed pro forma material relating to fictitious persons rather than any information on named individuals Mrs Doris Jackson of Heversham, Cumbria, was kind enough to give her permission to quote from documents in her possession. The author is grateful to Mr Peter Park for drawing this source to his attention.

Numerous colleagues within the Public Record Office have given support and encouragement during the compilation of this work. A special mention should be made of Mrs Beryl Saddington for undertaking the typing of a complex and frequently revised text with good humour and patience.

Edward Higgs

Public Record Office

July 1988

1 Introduction

This book is a guide to the manuscript census returns for the period 1801 to 1901, and can be used both as a general introduction and as a means of reference when working on the records. To this end each section is as self-contained as possible. It approaches the subject from an archival point of view to provide an administrative background to the census, to describe the documents in detail, and to comment on the nature and reliability of the information they contain. By taking the whole of the nineteenth century as the period of analysis, it can put the process of census-taking into a proper historical context.

The manuscript returns of the nineteenth-century censuses can be used in numerous ways to reconstruct the past. Information relating to individuals can be used by genealogists, biographers and those studying specific groups. The structure of families revealed in the census is of interest to historical demographers. The aggregation of these in communities can in turn be studied by local historians. Such studies through the census are also becoming increasingly common in schools. Lastly, historians of the social and economic structure of England and Wales use the census for national surveys, either through sampling the manuscript returns, through studies of contrasting communities, or by consulting the tables in the published *Census reports* derived from the former.

Since the censuses from 1841 onwards identify people by name it is also possible to link the information they contain with that from other documents; parish registers, certificates of births, marriages and deaths, and so on. This allows a much more exhaustive analysis of individuals, families and communities.

Given the importance of this source, it is essential that those intending to use it should understand its structure, and the meaning of the information it contains. This has not always been the case because the census has not been placed in its administrative and intellectual context. Nor have historians always had a firm grasp of the administrative procedures and technicalities of census-taking.

Other works have been written on nineteenth-century census-taking but these have concentrated as much on the published reports as on the manuscript returns.[1] By covering a very large area the authors have been forced to summarise or omit many of the findings of specialist studies scattered in journals and monographs. They are also as much

---

1   For the main published guides to the nineteenth-century censuses see the Office of Population Censuses and Surveys & General Register Office, Edinburgh, *Guide to census reports, Great Britain 1801–1966* (London, 1977); *The Census and social structure: an interpretative guide to nineteenth century censuses for England and Wales*, ed. R Lawton (London, 1978); and *Nineteenth-century society*, ed. E A Wrigley (Cambridge, 1972).

concerned with what one can do with census data as with what that information is. The focus is upon migration, for example, rather than upon the nature and reliability of birthplace data in the census. This no doubt reflects the background of the authors in historical research but reduces the usefulness of these works as means of reference when studying the records. Such works do not usually look in any detail at the censuses of 1801 to 1831, or discuss comprehensively the form of those of 1891 and 1901, the records of which are as yet closed to public inspection.

1901 has been chosen as a natural date to end this survey because of the changes introduced into the census-taking process in 1911. From 1841 to 1901 householders gave information regarding the members of their families on household schedules, and this information was copied into special books for dispatch to the census authorities in London. The data they contained was then digested and published in a series of parliamentary reports. The enumerators' books are the manuscript returns which have been preserved and are now available for public inspection at the Public Record Office (PRO) in London. In 1911, for the first time, only the original householders' schedules were forwarded to London, and abstraction and tabulation was done from these directly. The schedules were also more complex because of the introduction of new questions, especially some relating to marital fertility.

Although the taking of the census was a single administrative process for the whole of Great Britain until 1861, the present work is almost exclusively concerned with England and Wales. Because of differences in the legal, constitutional and administrative systems in Scotland, the censuses in the northern kingdom were always handled in a rather different manner. From 1861 onwards the taking of the census in Scotland was the responsibility of a separate registrar general for Scotland, and diverged from its counter-part south of the border in content and form. The separate Irish censuses, and the enumerations or headcounts taken in the colonies to coincide with the census of England and Wales, are also beyond the scope of this book.

Part I The historical and administrative background

2 The history of nineteenth-century census-taking

The state and population surveys

The central state in England has long been involved in surveying its resources in lands, goods and people. Domesday Book itself was an attempt to discover just such information for Anglo-Norman England. The records generated by later methods of taxation can also be used to calculate population size and structure. But such sources were never intended to give the authorities a comprehensive picture of the whole population. Domesday Book was essentially a survey of landholding. People were only mentioned as appendages to the land, and even then in an incomplete manner. The records of the poll and hearth taxes only related to people who paid the tax or to households. In order to calculate the total population it is necessary to estimate the extent of the unrecorded population, or to estimate average household size. Such difficulties arise from using these records as surrogates for population censuses. Much the same could also be said of similar records produced in other countries.

Such narrow pecuniary interests gradually gave way to broader considerations in the late seventeenth and eighteenth centuries. In this period European states and their colonies came to take stock of their military resources in an age of almost incessant warfare. Possibly the first attempt to count everyone in an area larger than a city at successive intervals was made in La Nouvelle France (Quebec) and Acadie (Nova Scotia), where sixteen enumerations were undertaken between 1665 and 1754. A complete census was taken in Iceland in 1703. In 1749 the Swedish clergy, who had long kept lists of parishioners, were required to render returns from which the total population of Sweden (including Finland) was obtained, and a similar exercise took place in Denmark in 1787. In Austria under the impact of Maria Theresa's population policy, partly a response to the effects of the Turkish wars, censuses were initiated in 1754. Various Italian states conducted approximately accurate enumerations in the eighteenth century: Sardinia in 1773 and 1795; Parma in 1770; and Tuscany in 1766. Enumerations also occurred in several German states from 1742 onwards.

Although some British colonies in America had made full enumerations in the period before the American War of Independence, the first census of the United States in 1790 broke new ground. This was not only because of the size of the area enumerated, and the attempt to obtain information on certain characteristics of individuals in the population, but also because of the political purpose for which it was undertaken: the apportionment of representation in Congress.[1]

Private estimates of the population of England date back at least to the works of William Petty, Gregory King and Charles Davenant in the late seventeenth century. A new population debate arose in the 1750s as to whether or not the population had increased since the Glorious Revolution of 1688.[2] Conservative defenders of the agricultural interest agreed with political radicals in believing that the population of England had declined under the dominance of a Whig aristocracy and the rising commercial classes. Commerce and political jobbery were seen as having caused a general moral and sexual debauchment which had led to population decline. Similar views were held by radicals such as William Cobbett in the early nineteenth century.[3] Others defended the rise of commerce and claimed that the population had increased since 1688. Much of this debate revolved around population estimates based upon taxation records and the ecclesiastical registers of baptisms, marriages and burials.

A new twist was given to the controversy by the publication in 1798 of Malthus's *Essay on the principle of population*. The full title of the 1803 edition was in fact an *Essay on the principle of population, or a view of its past and present effects on human happiness, with an enquiry into our prospects respecting the future removal or mitigation of the evils which it occasions*. The debate shifted from the effect of morality on population growth to the relationship between the latter and the available agricultural resources of society. If population grew according to a geometrical ratio (2, 4, 8, 16, 32, . . .), and agricultural production according to an arithmetic progression (1, 2, 3, 4, 5, . . .), at what point would population pressure encroach on social resources, and what would be the consequences?

A bill proposing an annual enumeration of the population by the overseers of the poor, and the enforcement of compulsory ecclesiastical registration of vital events, was introduced into parliament in 1753. Its supporters hoped that these measures would allow the calculation of the maximum size of any army which could be raised in times of need; provide evidence as to the desirability of emigration to the colonies; and show the burden of the poor law on the country. Its opponents argued that the proposed enumeration would be impractical and costly, and might be used as the basis of new taxation and conscription. Given the eighteenth-century perception of a standing army as the first step to the establishment of an absolute monarchy, the violence of the opposition to the bill is perhaps understandable. Memories of the attempt by James II to establish just such a government through an army loyal to the Crown, and to reintroduce Roman Catholicism, were still very much alive. Nevertheless, the bill passed through all its stages in the Commons and received its second reading in the Lords. It was, however, referred to a Committee of the Whole House, and before this could meet the parliamentary session ended and the bill lapsed.

1   *Encyclopaedia Britannica* (London, 1969); D V Glass, *Numbering the people: the eighteenth century population controversy and the development of census and vital statistics in Britain* (London, 1978), pp 12–13.
2   Glass, *Numbering the people*, pp 11–89.
3   W Cobbett, *Rural rides* (Harmondsworth, 1983), p 67.

The origins of the 1801 census

The inception of decennial census-taking in 1801 has been seen explicitly in terms of the particular conditions in the country in 1800 when the first Census Act was passed. The period was one of war, bad harvests and food shortages; a typical Malthusian crisis of subsistence. Large numbers of agricultural workers were also serving in the militia and so unable to work on the land. What could be more natural than the desire to enumerate the population in order to discover how many mouths needed to be fed, and how many were working to feed them?[4]

Aspects of the first census do indeed appear to confirm this hypothesis. Not only was an enumeration made of the total population but an attempt was made to divide it into three groups; those working in agriculture, those in trade, manufactures and handicrafts, and those in other employments. At the same time a separate agricultural survey to be performed by the clergymen of the parish was also initiated. The results of this survey, known as the Acreage Returns, show the number of acres in each parish devoted to differing crops and now form the record class HO 67 at the PRO.[5]

The 1800 Census Act (41 George III, cap. 15) was, however, explicitly called 'An Act for taking an Account of the Population of Great Britain, and the increase or diminution thereof', as were all the decennial Census Acts until that of 1840. As well as an enumeration of the population, an attempt was also made to obtain data on baptisms, marriages and burials for the whole of the eighteenth century. This indicates that the reasons for the inception of nineteenth-century census-taking should be sought in the general population controversies of the late eighteenth century.

It could be argued, moreover, that the role of the agricultural crisis was to facilitate enumeration rather than to instigate it. Since food prices were high in 1800–1, many of the poor were applying to the overseers of the poor for relief. This was usually granted according to the number of children maintained by each applicant, and the overseers would thus be in an excellent position to know the total numbers of people in their parishes.

Whatever the reasons for taking the first census in 1801, its history, and that of the next three enumerations, is intimately connected with the career of John Rickman. Rickman (1771–1840) was the son of a clergyman and conducted the *Commercial, Agricultural, and Manufacturer's Magazine* for some time after his graduation from Oxford in 1792. In 1796 he wrote a paper showing that it would be administratively easy and profitable to take a census of the population. The manuscript was shown to Charles Abbot (afterwards Lord Colchester) by George Rose, the member of parliament for Christchurch. Abbot hired Rickman as his secretary, and employed him in preparing the first Census Act, which Abbot introduced into Parliament in December 1800. When the latter became chief secretary for Ireland in 1801, Rickman went with him to Dublin, and was made deputy keeper of the privy seal. He refused a permanent appointment in Ireland, and when Abbot became speaker in February 1802, Rickman continued to be his secretary and settled in London. In July 1814 he was appointed second clerk assistant at the table of the House of

4   Glass, *Numbering the people*, pp 96–98.
5   Acreage Returns (PRO: HO 67).

Commons, and in 1820 clerk assistant, a position he held until his death. Rickman organised the administration of all the censuses from 1801 to 1831.[6]

The first four censuses carry all the hallmarks of central government prior to the 1832 Reform Act. The initiation of census-taking reflected the interest taken in the subject by an aristocratic grandee such as Colchester, and the enumerations depended for their organisation upon the work of one of his clients. The local administration of the census was based upon the officers of the Elizabethan poor law system and of the established church. With the changes in the structure of central and local government in the 1830s, new administrative methods and preoccupations were to develop.

Early census administration, 1801–1831

Since the administrative machinery established in 1801 remained the basis of subsequent enumerations until 1841, a description of the taking of the first census is of considerable interest.[7]

The schedule attached to the Census Act of 1800 contained the following questions:

1   How many inhabited houses are there in your parish, township, or place; by how many families are they occupied; and how many houses therein are uninhabited?

2   How many persons (including children of whatever age) are there actually found within the limits of your parish, township, or place, at the time of taking this account, distinguishing males and females, and exclusive of men actually serving in his majesty's regular forces or militia, and exclusive of seamen either in his majesty's service or belonging to registered vessels?

3   What number of persons in your parish, township, or place are chiefly employed in agriculture; how many in trade, manufactures, or handicraft; and how many are not occupied in any of the preceding classes?

4   What was the number of baptisms and burials in your parish, township, or place in the several years 1700, 1710, 1720, 1730, 1740, 1750, 1760, 1770, 1780, and in each subsequent year to the 31st December, 1800, distinguishing males from females?

5   What was the number of marriages in your parish, township, or place in each year, from the year 1754 inclusive to the end of the year 1800?

6   Are there any matters which you think it necessary to remark in explanation of your answers to any of the preceding questions?

In England and Wales the responsibility for answering the first five questions was divided. The first three were addressed to those responsible for making the enumeration by house to house enquiry on 10 March, 1801, or as soon as possible after that date. This duty was placed upon the overseers of the poor or 'other substantial householders'. The fourth and fifth questions were addressed to the clergy.

6   *Dictionary of national biography* (London, 1896).
7   For a more detailed discussion of early census administration see the Office of Population Censuses and Surveys & General Register Office, Edinburgh, *Guide to census reports*, pp 13–18.

The king's printer was instructed to send copies of the Act and schedule to clerks of the peace and town clerks, who were required to distribute them to the local justices of the peace. They were also required to deliver enough copies of the schedule to high constables, or 'other proper officers', so the latter could ensure that one copy was received by the overseer of the poor, or other substantial householder, and by the rector, vicar, curate, or other officiating minister in each parish, township or place.

All census returns had to be made on prescribed forms which were attached to the schedule of the Act. These merely asked for raw numbers. In order to make the returns the relevant officers were authorised 'to ask all such questions of the persons within the said parish, township, or place, respecting themselves and the number and quality of persons constituting the respective families, as shall be necessary for stating the particulars required to be stated concerning them, in the said answers and returns'.[8] This led some overseers to draw up nominal listings of the inhabitants of their parish from which the final returns were digested. In some areas local printers produced printed forms for this purpose, presumably based on Rickman's schedules. In London and elsewhere printed schedules were produced which were to be left with householders to fill up themselves. These subsidiary documents were retained locally amongst the poor law records, or in the parish chest. It is probable that some populous parishes were broken down into smaller districts and enumerated individually by differing parish officials.[9]

The official returns made by the enumerators had to be attested or affirmed before the justices of the peace on a day which they were authorised to fix between dates specified in the Act. In England and Wales the returns were then handed to the high constables or 'other proper officers' to be endorsed and submitted, together with a complete list of the names of enumerators, to the clerks of the peace or town clerks. These in turn were to send the returns to the Home Office not later than 15 May. There they were to be 'digested and reduced to order by such officer as such secretary of state (for the Home Department) shall appoint for the purpose'. Returns compiled from the parish registers had to be forwarded by the clergy to the bishop of the diocese, who was required to send them to his archbishop. Their final destination was the Privy Council. The preparation of the abstracts of the returns which were laid before Parliament was assigned to John Rickman, who signed the reports.

The overseers of the poor laid their accounts before the quarter sessions which could order their reimbursement out of the revenues collected by the receiver general of land taxes.[10] These orders were sent to the Exchequer and can be found in the record class E 182 at the PRO.[11] There appears to be some rough correlation between the number of families in a parish or township, as given in the *Census reports*, and the amounts paid out to the overseers.

In 1811 three important changes were introduced into the core questions asked at each census. The question concerning uninhabited houses was divided in order to distinguish

8   Census Act 1800 (41 Geo III, cap. 15), section 3.
9   P Laxton, 'Liverpool in 1801: manuscript return for the first national census of population', *Transactions of the Historical Society of Lancashire and Cheshire*, CXXX (1980), pp 76–79.
10   Census Act 1800 (41 Geo III, cap. 15), section 10.
11   Receivers' Accounts of Land and Assessed Taxes: Subsidiary Documents (PRO: E 182).

the number of houses being built from the number uninhabited for any other reason, such as dilapidation. The distinction was intended to give an indication of the degree of prosperity of the districts. The question relating to the occupations of individuals was modified to read 'What number of families (rather than persons) are chiefly employed in or maintained by' work in the three economic sectors of 1801. In the first census some male householders had included their female relatives, children and servants in the same occupational class as themselves, whilst others expressly excluded them. Lastly, the clergy were now asked to record the number of baptisms, marriages and burials registered in each of the previous ten years.[12]

Other questions were later asked on an ad hoc basis. In 1821 enumerators were asked to indicate, if the information could be obtained 'in a manner satisfactory to yourself, and not inconvenient to the parties', the number of males and females in five year age bands up to twenty years, and in ten year age bands thereafter. This attempt to gather information on age structure was partly in order to improve the life tables upon which life insurance schemes were based, and partly to establish the number of men able to bear arms.[13]

In 1831 much more extensive questions relating to occupations were asked. These appear to have reflected a desire to amass data on the economy which would refute potentially subversive economic theories such as the labour theory of value. The latter could imply that all wealth was created by members of the labouring classes.[14] The number of males 'upwards of twenty years' were to be given for seven economic categories. These were those employed: **1** in agriculture (subdivided into occupiers of land who employed labourers, other occupiers of land, and agricultural labourers); **2** in manufacture; **3** in retail trade or handicraft; **4** as capitalists, bankers, merchants and professionals; **5** as miners, fishermen, non-agricultural labourers, etc.; **6** those not included in the previous categories, such as the retired or disabled; and **7** those employed as servants. The number of male servants under twenty and the number of female servants was also to be given. Enumerators were also asked to give the trades of those employed in retailing and handicrafts, and indicate the numbers following them; the specific manufactures employing those in the second category; and the specific numbers in the various occupational groups in the fifth category. The clergy were also asked to indicate the number of illegitimate children born in their parish in 1830.

1841: the transition to modern census-taking

With hindsight the course of history can seem a logical and inevitable progression. The transfer of responsibility for census-taking to the General Register Office (GRO) in 1840, and the establishment of the means of enumerating the population which have lasted until the present day, can be seen in this light. A detailed examination of the circumstances

---

12   *1811 census report: abstract of the answers and returns*, PP 1812 XI [316 & 317], pp ix–x; Census Act 1811 (51 Geo III, cap. 6), Schedule.

13   Census Act 1820 (1 Geo IV, cap. 94), Schedule; *Minutes of evidence taken (session 1830) before the select committee on the Population Bill*, PP 1840 XV [396], pp 6–7, 25–27.

14   *Minutes of evidence taken (session 1830) before the select committee on the Population Bill*, p 7; Census Act 1830; (11 Geo IV, cap. 30), Schedule.

under which the 1841 census was taken, however, reveals a far more complicated picture. Indeed, the 1841 enumeration was a rather ad hoc affair and very much a transitional stage between Rickman's censuses and the mature Victorian censuses from 1851 onwards. This explains some of the peculiarities of the 1841 returns.

The 1830s certainly saw the development of the administrative machinery which was to take over the census in 1841. This reflected the reform of the central state after the broadening of the electoral base by the 1832 Reform Act. The Poor Law Amendment Act of 1834 created the union as the general unit of poor law administration, and this new administrative unit was adopted first for the civil registration of births, marriages and deaths, and then for census purposes. The Municipal Corporations Act of 1835 paved the way for the creation of a new order of local government officials who were to become the backbone of the enumerating class. Finally, the Births and Deaths Registration Act of 1836, providing for the compulsory civil registration of births, marriages and deaths, created a new system of central and local administration which was to be the basis of census-taking from 1841 onwards. The gathering of information on vital events from the records of ecclesiastical registration had always been part of Rickman's censuses: what could have been more natural than that the rest of the census process should be undertaken by this new registration machinery?[15]

In the wake of the 1836 Act a registrar general was appointed as head of the national system of civil registration. This officer had a central staff in the GRO whose task was to prepare reports and summary statistics on vital events from data collected locally. The whole country was divided up into registration districts, based upon the poor law unions, and a superintendent registrar appointed for each. These areas were further subdivided into sub-districts and part-time registrars appointed to them. These officers, often local doctors, were responsible for the registration of births, marriages and deaths within their sub-districts, and the forwarding of this information to the GRO in London. All that was necessary to turn this into an administrative system for the collection of census data was for the registrars to divide their sub-districts into smaller enumeration districts and to appoint a temporary enumerator for each. The latter could collect the necessary information which would be sent via the registrar and superintendent registrar to the GRO for central processing in the same manner as data on vital events.

There was certainly public pressure building up in the late 1830s for a much more ambitious census. The London (later Royal) Statistical Society had set up a committee to make recommendations on the 1841 census, and its report suggested a radical change in the organisation of the census to take advantage of the new poor law and civil registration systems. The members of the committee advocated the use of an official household schedule listing each individual by name, and giving their characteristics. These were to be transcribed into books by the enumerators for dispatch to London. They also advocated a much greater range of questions relating to age, sex, marital status, occupation, place of birth, religion and health. This 'blunderbuss' approach to data collection was typical of the statistical movement which was so widespread in this period. Eventually many of their

---

15   For a history of the GRO see M Nissel, *People count: a history of the General Register Office* (London, 1987).

recommendations were incorporated into the 1841 census, although the range of questions asked was much diminished.[16]

In reality, however, the transition to the new system of census-taking was far from inevitable, or straightforward. John Rickman appears to have been fully involved in the early preparations for taking the census in 1841. In 1836 he had forwarded circulars to the local clergy for the purposes of gathering information as far back as 1570 from the parish registers. He had abstracted the results and hoped to publish these in order to show population trends from the sixteenth century onwards. He was also responsible for drawing up a draft Census Bill on the lines of previous censuses, and had been examining the possibility of using the boundaries and officers of the new poor law to gather information. Rickman appears to have been in charge of these preparations until approximately 11 June 1840, when he fell ill from a throat infection from which he eventually died in August of that year. It was only in the last week of June that the Home Office discussed the taking of the census with John Lister, the first registrar general.[17]

Lister drew up a new bill which was the basis of the first Census Act for the 1841 census (3 & 4 Victoria, cap. 99). This Act, although containing many of the recommendations of the London Statistical Society, also had certain similarities with Rickman's enumerations. The local gathering of information was to be the duty of temporary enumerators appointed by the local registrar. They were to gather a much wider range of data on the characteristics of the individual members of the population of their district. This was to be done on one night in the year rather than as previously over a period of time. The census was to be a 'snapshot' of society at one moment in time so as to avoid the problems of double counting as people moved from parish to parish.

Lister envisaged at this point, however, that the enumerators would gather this information themselves by house to house enquiries as in previous censuses. The clergy were also to be asked to give the usual information from the parish registers and a schedule for that purpose was appended to the Act. In the end this information was not gathered, although the results of Rickman's analysis of parish register data from 1570 onwards eventually formed part of the *1841 census report*.[18]

Lister did not like household schedules because he believed that most householders were too illiterate to fill them in properly. He only appears to have countenanced their introduction after a pilot enumeration in London had shown how many enumerators would have to be employed to gather the data by door to door enquiries. The use of household schedules had to be hastily authorised by a supplementary Census Act (4 & 5 Victoria, cap. 7) which was passed only some two months before the enumeration was due to take place.

16   M J Cullen, *The statistical movement in early Victorian Britain: the foundations of empirical social research* (Hassocks, 1975), pp 96–97; D V Glass & P A M Taylor, *Population and emigration: government and society in nineteenth century Britain* (Dublin, 1976), pp 14–15.

17   Treasury Board Papers (PRO: T 1): T 1/4573, 10 Feb 1841, Wm Rickman *et al* to C G Trevelyan [presumably E C Trevelyan, assistant secretary at the Treasury]; Census Returns: Specimens of Forms and Documents (PRO: RG 27): RG 27/1, p 1.

18   RG 27/1, pp 6–11; *Parish registers* (London, 1845).

Nor was the connection with officers of the Palace of Westminster severed at this date. The 1841 census was to be administered by three census commissioners; Lister, Edmund Phipps, about whom little is known, and Thomas Vardon, who was librarian of the House of Commons, and had some experience of census-taking in 1831. Lister died in 1842, before the end of the census-abstracting process, and it was left to Vardon and Phipps to sign the final report.[19]

The rather ad hoc nature of the transition of census-taking to the GRO, and the limited amount of time Lister had to plan the 1841 census, are reflected in the idiosyncratic nature of the 1841 returns. They are certainly rather different from those of later enumerations. Lister was anxious to produce as simple a household schedule as possible and kept the heads of information gathered to a minimum. These included name, age (rounded down to the nearest term of five if over fourteen years), sex, 'profession, trade, employment or of independent means', whether born in the same county (yes or no), or whether born in Scotland, Ireland or 'foreign parts'. Later censuses, on the other hand, sought additional information on relationship to head of household, marital condition, full ages, the exact place of birth, and details of medical disabilities.

Nor were some of the 'problem' groups, for which special arrangements were made in later censuses, catered for in the administration of the 1841 census. The schedule designed specifically for the crew of merchant vessels, for example, only appeared in 1851. Similarly, no special arrangements were made for recording nightworkers in 1841. Also, many of the detailed instructions given to enumerators and householders in later censuses were not distributed in 1841. Although the enumerator was instructed to leave a household schedule with each householder, for example, the latter was not told if lodgers and boarders were to be counted as part of his or her 'family'. As one might expect, the accumulation of practical experience led to the gradual perfection of the census-taking machinery.

A final difference between 1841 and the later censuses under the GRO was that in the former the principal population tables in the published reports gave the population for each ancient county, and within these for the traditional administrative units; hundreds, wapentakes, sokes, liberties and parishes. This was plainly to make the tables comparable with those in the earlier *Census reports*. From 1851 onwards the main units used were the registration counties (not always the same as the ancient counties), registration districts, sub-districts, parishes and townships.

All these factors make it difficult to compare information in the 1841 census with much of that collected in later years.

Taking a mid-Victorian census

The nineteenth-century censuses from 1851 onwards followed a common administrative pattern. A general description of this census-taking machinery helps to reveal its strengths and weaknesses.

---

19   RG 27/1, pp 11–18; Home Office: Registered Files (PRO: HO 45): HO 45/146, 10 Jan 1845, Phipps and Vardon to Phillipps; *1841 census report: abstract of the answers and returns*, PP 1844 XXVII [587], p 72.

The first step taken by the GRO was to approach its parent department (the Home Office prior to 1871 and the Local Government Board thereafter) to get the necessary Census Act passed by Parliament. This authorised the questions to be asked and the disbursement of central government funds for the establishment of the census-taking apparatus.

The process of negotiation with other departments and outside bodies over the information to be sought could be protracted and difficult. There was a constant tension between the GRO's desire to keep the household schedule as simple as possible, and the desire of bodies such as the Royal Statistical Society to ask questions which were of burning interest to them.

Having obtained sanction for expenditure on the census, the GRO had to remind local officers of their duties, design and print household schedules and instruction books, and set up a central Census Office for processing the local returns. This involved hiring temporary clerks via the Treasury, training them, finding a suitable building in which to house them, arranging with the Metropolitan Police for night security, and so on. All this had to be done from scratch every ten years since the nineteenth-century Census Acts only sanctioned expenditure for the local collection of data, its central processing and the publication of reports. This process only took some three or four years. The Census Office did not become a permanent institution until well into the present century. This work also had to be done at great speed since the Census Acts were usually passed only some seven or eight months before the night of the census.[20]

Nor should one imagine that the organisation of census-taking at the local level was an effortless process.[21] The local registrars had to advise the GRO on any changes to local administrative boundaries, which could be legion. They also had to forward to London a list of all institutions in their district with the number of their inmates. If over a certain size, these were to be enumerated separately by the chief residing officer.

The local registrars were also supposed to revise their plans of division. These were documents, copies of which were held both locally and at the GRO, which defined the enumeration districts into which each registration sub-district was divided for the purposes of census-taking. The 'plans' were written descriptions of the districts rather than maps, which had been drawn up in 1841 on fairly rational principles. The registration districts were, at that period, meaningful administrative entities, being co-extensive with the new poor law unions of 1834. These were in turn subdivided into districts for enumeration such that each should contain in towns no more than about 200 inhabited houses. The number depended, however, on the distance which the enumerators would

---

20   For the steps involved in setting up the local and central census-taking apparatus in 1891, see the General Register Office Letter Books (PRO: RG 29): RG 29/9–16. It is a mistake to assume that there was a permanent Census Office, as in M Conk, 'Labor statistics in the American and English census: making some invidious comparisons', *Journal of Social History*, XVI (1982–1983), pp 83–102.

21   Much of the following description of census-taking has been derived from the instruction books circulated to the registrars and enumerators prior to census day: 1841, RG 27/1, pp 18–35; 1851, HO 45/3579; 1861, RG 27/3, Items 11–14; 1871, RG 27/4, Item 29; 1881, RG 27/5, Item 27; 1891, RG 27/6, Item 6. At the time that these records were transferred to the PRO, the volume in this series for 1901 was recorded as being 'Wanting'. The instructions for the officers taking the 1901 census in the Islands in the British Seas (the Isle of Man and the Channel Islands) can be found in the Census Returns: Correspondence and Papers (PRO: RG 19): RG 19/23.

have to travel; an enumeration district in the countryside contained fewer houses than in the town. Many registrars failed to change these plans from census to census and they became hopelessly out of date. The boundaries of numerous enumeration districts were not altered in line with local administrative changes, while changes in the density of population caused ever wider variations in the numbers of households in an enumeration district.

Once this basic ground work had been laid, the local registrars selected an enumerator for each enumeration district. They could appoint whoever they liked as long as they met the basic requirements:

> He must be a person of intelligence and activity; he must read and write well, and have some knowledge of arithmetic; he must not be infirm or of such weak health as may render him unable to undergo the requisite exertion; he should not be younger than 18 years of age or older than 65; he must be temperate, orderly and respectable, and be such a person as is likely to conduct himself with strict propriety, and to deserve the goodwill of the inhabitants of his district.

Enumerators were usually paid a fixed sum, and then so much for every 100 persons above 400 enumerated, plus so much for excess travelling. In 1871, for example, the enumerators were paid a fixed fee of one guinea; 2s.6d. for every 100 persons in their district above the first 400 enumerated; 6d. for every mile above the first five miles covered in delivering schedules; and 6d. for every mile above the first five miles covered in collecting schedules. It was almost universally agreed that these rates of pay were insufficient in themselves to attract high quality staff, or to encourage the greatest diligence.[22] The GRO pinned its hopes on attracting men of local standing who would undertake the work as a social duty. In the towns the registrars appear to have depended on local government officers but in the countryside they must have fallen back on the help of farmers and schoolteachers. The enumerators could employ an assistant out of their own pocket to deliver schedules and the like, although there is no direct evidence of how many did so.

In rural areas the enumerator might well have considerable local knowledge. In the case of Crosby Ravensworth in Westmorland in 1861 the enumerator was the local schoolmaster, John Sutherland, who had also officiated in 1841 and 1851. Sutherland's diary for the period shows him attending the parish council, collecting tithes and church rates, filling out income tax forms and witnessing wills for neighbours, as well as collecting census returns. He also drew up his own private census of the parish in a printed book based on the form of the census returns. The latter had a column for remarks in which he noted in later years the subsequent marriages, deaths and migration of the people he had enumerated in the census. It is plain that Sutherland was thoroughly acquainted with the inhabitants of his parish but it is unlikely that such an intimate system of surveillance would have been so common in large cities.[23]

22   E Higgs, 'The struggle for the occupational census, 1841–1911', in *Government and expertise: specialists, administrators and professionals, 1860–1914*, ed. R M MacLeod (Cambridge, 1988), pp 83–84.

23   Sutherland's diary and his 1861 census book are in the possession of his descendant Mrs Doris Jackson of Birk Nott, Heversham, Cumbria. Other returns, compiled by Sutherland in 1861 and 1871, can be found at the Cumbria Record Office (Kendal) amongst the Crosby Ravensworth parish records: Crosby Ravensworth Parish Records (Cumbria Record Office (Kendal): WPR/7): WPR/7/Misc. The author would like to thank Mr Peter Park for drawing these records to his attention.

Each enumerator was supplied by the registrar with a set of household schedules, an enumerator's book, and an instruction and memorandum book. In 1871, for example, the latter contained columns for addresses, types of houses (private, public, shops, uninhabited, etc.), the numbers of household schedules left and collected at each house, and a column for notes. There were also spaces for recording the numbers of people temporarily present or absent from the district. The enumerator used the book to order the houses, to mark down where houses were being built or were uninhabited, and to keep a check on whether or not he had collected all the schedules distributed. These records do not appear to have been sent to the GRO, and consequently have not found their way into the PRO.[24]

The enumerator left a household schedule with each householder. This gave instructions to the latter on how to enter the details required on each individual in the household on census night. This was usually in March or April in order to avoid the distortions in the data which would be caused by the seasonal movements of sections of the population during the summer. The information sought until 1891 for each household was the address where its members lived and, for each person within it, name, marital status, relationship to the household head, age, sex, 'Rank, profession or occupation', parish and county of birth, and descriptions of medical disabilities.[25]

On the morning after census night the enumerator collected the schedules. If these were not completed properly he was supposed to ask for extra details on the doorstep, although there is considerable evidence that this was not done uniformly. If the householder was unable to fill in the schedule, perhaps because he or she was illiterate, the enumerator was to fill it in for them. The proportion of schedules which had to be filled out in this manner must have varied from district to district. In 1871 enumerators were asked to record the number of schedules they filled in themselves on the page in their enumeration books given over to summary tables. In parts of Manchester the proportion so completed was twenty-five per cent; in Christ Church, Spitalfields the proportion was fifteen per cent; in Colyton in Devon it was seven per cent; but in some Welsh speaking parishes in Anglesey the majority were filled in by the enumerators.[26] It is not possible to gauge the proportion of the schedules which had to be filled out for householders by their neighbours.

The enumerators then copied the household schedules into their enumerators' books, taking care to distinguish between houses and the differing households they contained. In the process of doing so some enumerators tended to standardise the information in the household schedules. They were also to fill in the tables at the front of the books giving the numbers of houses and persons on each page, and the number of persons temporarily present or absent. The books were supposed to be checked by the registrars and superintendent registrars before dispatch to the Census Office in London but this seldom

---

24   Blank examples of these memorandum books can be found in the PRO record class RG 27: 1861, RG 27/3, Item 17; 1871, RG 27/4, Item 28; 1881, RG 27/5, Item 26; 1891, RG 27/6, Item 70.

25   Examples of the household schedules can be found in various PRO record classes: 1841, RG 27/1, pp 56–57; 1851, HO 45/3579; 1861, RG 27/3, Item 2; 1871, RG 27/4, Item 5; 1881, RG 27/5, Item 5; 1891, RG 27/6, Item 68; 1901, RG 19/11.

26   1871 Census Returns (PRO: RG 10): Christ Church, Spitalfields, RG 10/505–511; Colyton, RG 10/2035–2036; Llanallgo and Llangwyllog, Anglesey, RG 10/5742. For Manchester see, P Rushton, 'Anomalies as evidence in nineteenth-century censuses', *Local Historian*, XIII (1978–1979), p 483.

appears to have been done. The householders' schedules were also sent to London at the same time.

In the Census Office the books were gone over again to sort out any problems or ambiguities in the data, reference no doubt being made to the household schedules. The clerks sometimes altered entries in the books and almost invariably corrected the enumerators' addition in the tables. Individual clerks then went through the books abstracting particular heads of information for the published tables. One would deal with ages, another with birthplaces, and so on. In the process of doing so they often ticked the items of information they were dealing with to ensure that no entries were omitted. At the end of this process the household returns appear to have been destroyed.[27]

Certain groups were enumerated separately for administrative convenience. As was noted above, inmates of institutions of a certain size were recorded by the chief resident officer on special institutional schedules.[28] Customs officers gave the masters of ships in port on census night, or who arrived in port within a stipulated period, a ships' schedule in which they were to record the members of the ship's crew and passengers.[29] The Admiralty handled the dispatch of special enumeration books to every ship in the Royal Navy, whilst the War Office provided a headcount of soldiers serving abroad.[30] These officers or bodies sent the schedules or books they collected directly to London, where they were amalgamated with the enumerators' books for the same locality for abstraction. In the case of shipping this could have bizarre effects on the published population tables for particular localities. The crew and passengers on a ship could be added to the population of a village simply because the ship was offshore on census night.[31]

It is important to recognise the comparatively short period of time in which the GRO had to organise the taking of the census, and the relatively poor quality of some of the agents involved; illiterate householders, slap-dash enumerators, and registrars who did not supervise the work properly. This explains, in part, why the GRO was so anxious to keep the census as simple as possible. It also alerts one to the problematical nature of some of the data in the manuscript returns. The information in the enumerators' books was several stages removed from reality, and each stage could add its own accumulation of errors. Did householders and enumerators always understand what was asked of them? Did they have to. make a guess as to the information to be supplied under certain headings? Did

27   There appears to be no record of their subsequent retention, or of their transfer to the PRO. They were certainly all destroyed by 1913; *Evidence and index to the second report of the Royal Commission on Public Records, Vol II, Pt III*, PP 1914 XLVI [Cd. 7456], Q 5570.

28   Examples of the institutional books can be found in various PRO record classes: 1841 and 1851, 1841 and 1851 Census Returns (PRO: HO 107); 1861, RG 27/3, Item 18; 1871, RG 27/4, Item 23; 1881, RG 27/5, Item 21; 1891, RG 27/6, Item 68; 1901, RG 19/11.

29   Examples of the merchant ships' schedules can be found in various PRO classes: 1851, HO 45/3579; 1861, RG 27/3, Item 40; 1871, RG 27/4, Items 8 & 9; 1881, RG 27/5, Items 8 & 9; 1891, RG 27/6, Item 67; 1901, RG 19/11. A ships' schedule does not appear to have been produced in 1841.

30   Examples of the Royal Navy ships' schedules can be found in the PRO record class RG 27: 1861, RG 27/3, Item 45; 1871, RG 27/4, Item 24; 1881, RG 27/5, Item 22; 1891, RG 27/6, Item 76. No schedule appears to have been issued in 1841. There is evidence that one was used in 1851 (see Chapter 7) but no examples appear to have survived. The 1901 census returns are closed to public inspection but the Royal Navy schedule used in 1901 was probably similar to that of 1891 (see RG 19/20, 15 Dec 1900, GRO draft letter to the Admiralty).

31   V C Burton, 'A floating population: vessel enumeration returns in censuses, 1851–1921', *Local Population Studies*, XXXVIII (1987), pp 36–43.

enumerators always understand what was told to them by illiterate, and perhaps suspicious, householders? What errors or omissions were made by the enumerators in the process of copying the household schedules into their books?

In general the work appears to have been done conscientiously but users must be aware of the failings of particular enumerators, local peculiarities and the problems associated with the interpretation of certain types of information.

The changing intellectual background to census-taking

An obvious question about this process, which is seldom asked, is what was the purpose to which this information was to be put? Strangely, there appear to be few examples of the data collected being used for central policy making until the end of the nineteenth century. The mid-century was certainly a period when the almost indiscriminate collection of statistics had become a mania, and the census can be seen as part of this movement to reveal the 'state of the nation'. The belief that certain laws, which were discoverable by empirical research, underlay creation was a very powerful strand in the intellectual makeup of the period. Thus, iron laws were said to underlie the workings of the free-market economy which were seen as ensuring a fair distribution of wealth. Opposition to the existing economic system must, it was believed, reflect ignorance or unreason. The collection of occupational data could serve, therefore, to reveal the true structure of the economy and so dispel radical discontent.[32]

It is perhaps most useful, however, to see the mid-nineteenth-century censuses in terms of medical surveys. Given the sort of information gathered this might seem a rather surprising suggestion, but it only becomes so if one looks back at early Victorian medicine from the perspective of the present century.

The central figure in the elaboration and administration of the mid-nineteenth-century censuses (1851–1871) was William Farr, the GRO's redoubtable superintendent of statistics from 1838 till his retirement in 1880. Farr was a commissioner for the censuses of 1851, 1861 and 1871, and was said to have written the *Census reports* of those years. He was certainly the main intellectual force within the Office. Farr came from a medical background and his most important work involved using the data obtained from the civil registration of deaths to plot the incidence and developmental laws of epidemic diseases. Farr was probably the greatest medical statistician of the century, and his work was of great importance for the public health and sanitation movements of the period.[33]

Farr's paradigm for the spread and nature of disease was based on chemistry. The biological germ theory did not gain general acceptance in this country until the 1870s or later. He saw disease as being caused by the intake of various chemicals into the blood causing a process of chemical change which poisoned the system. Such chemicals could enter the body in the form of dust particles, as noxious fumes, suspended in water, and so on. But in common with other sanitarians of the age, he saw the primary source of such

---

32   For the background to this statistical movement see Cullen, *The statistical movement in early Victorian Britain*.

33   For an introduction to Farr's life and work see, J M Eyler, *Victorian social medicine: the ideas and methods of William Farr* (London, 1979).

chemicals as being the concentrations of human effluent in large cities, the result of the rapid urbanisation of the population. The more people in the given area, the higher, Farr reasoned, would be the level of mortality. This theory was one of the intellectual underpinnings of the movement to revolutionise the sanitary arrangements of the great cities.[34]

This explains why the GRO not only wanted to know the overall size of the population but also the number of people in particular areas: hence the importance of knowing the population of defined administrative units, health being seen as in an inverse relationship to population density. At the simplest level, local medical officers of health needed to know the number of people in their districts so that they could calculate the number of deaths per 1,000 population, the universal measure of salubrity. This would also explain the interest in the formation of households, age, and marital status, which were seen as determinants of population growth, and in migration, the mechanism by which population was concentrated in cities. Even the questions relating to occupations can be seen in this light. The census schedules made a specific point of asking householders not only to give the occupations of the members of their households but also the materials upon which they worked. Farr appears to have believed that the material worked upon affected the character and life expectancy of workers, and he sought to use the data collected to construct occupational life-tables. The medical paradigm certainly did not exhaust the reasons for taking the census but it explains many of the features of the process.[35]

In this light it is interesting to examine the treatment of the data collected in the last column of the household schedule, that relating to medical disabilities. This column is usually ignored by historians but was plainly of great importance to the GRO. In the *1861 census report* the largest section of the commentary, nearly a third of the whole report, was given over to an analysis of the contents of this column. This was despite the universal recognition that the information gathered on blindness and the deaf and dumb was highly unreliable and incomplete.[36] The only example of a follow-up survey in the history of the nineteenth-century censuses was in this year, when the GRO found time to check the results of the returns of the blind and deaf and dumb by asking more detailed questions of those so afflicted in Herefordshire.[37] Between 1851 and 1891 the only major innovation introduced into the census schedule was the addition to this column of questions relating to the imbecility, idiocy or lunacy of household members; an enquiry which was hardly likely to produce very accurate data.

In the later nineteenth century the intellectual climate changed and with it the type of material collected. Farr retired in 1880 and none of his nineteenth-century successors achieved his standing in the statistical community. With the gradual triumph of the germ theory of disease, improvements in sanitation, and the decline in the death rate and the

34   Eyler, *Victorian social medicine*, pp 97–108.
35   E Higgs, 'The census as a medical survey, 1841–1911', a paper read on 27 November 1987 before the Wellcome Symposium on the History of Medicine on 'The General Register Office in the Nineteenth Century: a Comparative Perspective'.
36   *1861 census report*, PP 1863 LIII Pt 1 [3221].
37   *1861 census report*, pp 48–50. No returns from the survey appear to have survived.

rate of population growth, Farr's demographic and chemical paradigm for illness ceased to have much relevance. In the same period the rise of foreign economic competition during the Great Depression, eugenicist concern over the differential reproduction of the various classes in society, and a perceived heightening of class tensions, led to a greater interest in the economic and social structure of the nation. This applied not only to economists and sociologists, such as Charles Booth, but to government departments such as the Board of Trade and the Home Office.[38]

In 1891 a question on whether a person was an employer, an employee, or self-employed was introduced on the recommendation of the 1890 Treasury Committee on the Census. In the same year the number of rooms occupied by a household was to be given if the number was less than five. This was plainly linked to efforts to measure levels of overcrowding for the purposes of housing improvement. But this in turn could be seen as a medical matter since overcrowding and insanitary conditions were seen as inextricably linked. A decade later the Home Office had a question added relating to whether or not a person was working at home. This was to allow the effective administration of the Factory Acts. The only additional information sought in the census prior to 1911 was the incidence of Welsh-speaking in Wales from 1891 onwards.[39]

An examination of the history of the nineteenth-century censuses raises questions about the reliability of the information in the returns, and the comparability of the data between censuses. As the census-taking machinery was elaborated, and as the reasons for collecting the data changed, so did the instructions to householders and enumerators. An understanding of these changes is crucial to those wishing to use the censuses to compare the nation or specific communities over time. Part III contains a more detailed discussion of these matters.

38   Higgs, 'The struggle for the occupational census', pp 78–82.
39   Higgs, 'The struggle for the occupational census', p 83.

3   The archival history of the documents

The fate of the pre-1841 returns

As was noted above, two types of record were created in the process of taking the first four censuses. There were first the official returns on printed forms sent to John Rickman in London. These merely gave the number of people in the parish, the number of individuals or families in certain broad economic categories, the number of vital events in parish registers, and so on. The second type of record produced were the more detailed enumerations made by the local overseers of the poor in preparation for filling out their official returns. These were never intended to be sent to Rickman and found their way into the local poor law records or the parish chest, and from thence into local record offices and libraries.

Exactly what happened to the official returns after Rickman had finished with them is not certain. There is evidence that Rickman retained some of them in his own possession.[1] By 1846, however, they were reported to have been deposited in the Tower. Suggestions that they should be transferred to the vaults of the House of Commons followed but by 1862 they were in the new repository of the Public Record Office at Chancery Lane.[2]

Little attention appears to have been given to them so long as pressure on space at Chancery Lane was not serious. Towards the end of the century, however, the increasing accessions of modern departmental records began to make themselves felt. It became necessary to review the material which had flooded into the Office directly after its creation, much of which had been accepted without any attempt at proper archival selection.

In 1904 the PRO's inspecting officers, led by Sir Henry Maxwell-Lyte, and a Home Office representative, reviewed the census returns for 1801 to 1831. They recommended that these should be destroyed since most of their contents had been reproduced verbatim in the published *Census reports*.[3] The only real losses were probably the parish-level data on baptisms, burials and marriages, and the numbers of males aged twenty years and over in 100 named retail and handicraft occupations which were returned on a 'Formula for entry of males upwards of twenty years of age, employed in retail trade, or handicraft' for each

---

1   T 1/4753, Schedule of papers in custody of the ex[ecut]ors of the late John Rickman.
2   *Seventh report of the deputy keeper of the public records* (London, 1846), p 4; *Thirteenth report of the deputy keeper of the public records* (London, 1852), pp 2–3; *Twenty-fourth report of the deputy keeper of the public records* (London, 1863), p iv.
3   Public Record Office: Inspecting Officers' Committee: Correspondence and Papers (PRO: PRO 17): PRO 17/1, Home Office destruction schedule, 31 May 1904.

parish in 1831. In the published report the registration data was only given in an aggregated form for hundreds, and that returned on the Formula by counties. On the other hand, given the uncertain archival history of the early census records before they came into the PRO, one cannot be certain that this material was extant in 1904. The only centrally held records from the early censuses which were not destroyed were the clergymen's returns of 1831. These now form record class HO 71 at the PRO.[4]

It is quite erroneous to suggest that in 1904 the PRO destroyed nominal records similar to those of the post-1831 censuses, or even, as some historians believe, the household schedules of the later enumerations.[5] The former were never held centrally, and the latter were probably destroyed by the Census Office after they had been used to check the enumerators' books. Nor did the pre-1841 returns survive until 1931, as still others have claimed.[6]

The archival history of the post-1831 returns

Much of the archival history of the post–1831 returns is extremely obscure. As early as 1845 the registrar general was negotiating for the transfer of the 1841 returns to the PRO. These discussions proved abortive because the GRO would not undertake to box and list the documents. Similar negotiations were undertaken in 1852 with respect to the returns of 1841 and 1851. These appear to have only related to the enumerators' books and there is no direct evidence of any intention to transfer the household schedules which had probably already been destroyed. Eventually, by 1854, the enumerators' books for the 1851 census were deposited in the PRO.[7]

In 1859 the registrar general and the PRO entered into an extremely obscure correspondence on the subject of the storage of census records. The registrar general began by offering the PRO a further instalment of census returns. These may have been the returns of 1841. By the end of the year he was asking for the 1851 returns to be sent back to the GRO for consultation in preparation for abstracting the data from the 1861 enumerators' books. By 1862 the PRO appears to have had the returns of 1801 to 1841 in its safekeeping.[8]

The question of the PRO receiving custody of the enumerators' books did not arise again until 1903. In that year the GRO offered the PRO the 1871 and 1881 returns in order to make room for the 1901 books. The PRO refused to take them unless the GRO also transferred the earlier enumerators' returns. In the following year the 1841 and 1861 returns were found in the roof of the Houses of Parliament in the custody of the Office of Works. The 1851 books could not be found and were presumed lost. At what point the 1841 returns had been removed from the safekeeping of the PRO is difficult to determine. The PRO again

4   1831 Census, Clergyman's Returns (PRO: HO 71).

5   R Lawton, 'Introduction', in *The census and social structure*, ed. Lawton, p 16.

6   M Drake, 'The census, 1801–1891', in *Nineteenth-century society*, ed. Wrigley, p 31.

7   *Seventh report of the deputy keeper*, p 4; *Eighth report of the deputy keeper of the public records* (London, 1847) p 2; *Fifteenth report of the deputy keeper of the public records* (London, 1854), p 19.

8   Public Record Office, General Correspondence (PRO: PRO 1): PRO 1/23, 7 Feb 1859, George Graham to Sir F Palgrave; PRO 1/23, 16 March 1857 (attached to correspondence of 7 Feb 1859), George Graham to Sir Francis Palgrave; PRO 1/23, 20 July 1859, George Graham to Sir Francis Palgrave; PRO 1/23, 15 Dec 1859, George Graham to Sir Francis Palgrave; *Twenty-fourth report of the deputy keeper*, p iv.

refused to take the later returns unless it received the earlier records as well and put the onus on the Office of Works to find storage space for them. By 1912 the 1851 enumerators' returns had been found and were transferred, along with the 1841 books, to the PRO. The 1841 returns were said to be 'somewhat disarranged'.[9]

The later books were kept by the GRO for the purpose of ascertaining the ages of claimants to old age pensions. It was not until 1962 that the 1861 returns came into the PRO. The rest of the nineteenth-century enumerators' books, however, had all been deposited with the PRO by 1974.[10]

Plainly the nineteenth-century census returns have not always been stored and administered in optimum archival conditions. It should not be a surprise to discover that some of the earlier returns have been damaged, and even portions lost.

Public access to the census returns

The PRO administers records in conformity with the Public Records Acts of 1958 and 1967. Under these Acts public records selected for permanent preservation are normally opened to public inspection in the PRO in the January after they become thirty years old. With the approval of the lord chancellor, however, certain records may be withheld from public inspection after thirty years have elapsed under section 5(1) of the Public Records Act 1958, as amended by the 1967 Act. Before the lord chancellor gives his approval, he requires departments to satisfy him that the grounds for such closures conform to certain criteria. These are:

> exceptionally sensitive papers, the disclosure of which would be contrary to the public interest whether on security or other grounds (including the need to safeguard the Revenue);

> documents containing information supplied in confidence, the disclosure of which would or might constitute a breach of good faith;

> documents containing information about individuals, the disclosure of which would cause distress to or endanger living persons or their immediate descendants.

The census returns are closed for 100 years on the grounds that the information was supplied in confidence and its disclosure would be a breach of good faith. This means that the enumerators' books for the 1881 census are the latest that are currently open to public inspection. The 1891 returns will be opened in January 1992.[11]

---

9   PRO 1/68, 14 March 1903, A Mundy to PRO; PRO 1/68, 17 March 1903, S R Scargill-Bird to the registrar general; PRO 1/69, 19 Jan 1904, A Mundy to the deputy keeper of the public records; PRO 1/69, 15 April 1904, S R Scargill-Bird to the registrar general; PRO 1/77, 7 March 1912, W I Jerred to the Treasury; PRO 1/77, 13 May 1912, R A Roberts to H J Comyns.

10   *Fourth annual report of the keeper of the public records* (London, 1963), p 15; *Eighth annual report of the keeper of the public records* (London, 1967), p 19; *Eleventh annual report of the keeper of the public records* (London, 1970), p 19; *Thirteenth annual report of the keeper of the public records* (London, 1972), p 21; *Sixteenth annual report of the keeper of the public records* (London, 1975), p 16.

11   The subject of access to public records is discussed in a leaflet available from the PRO entitled 'Access to public records'.

Part II   The structure of the records

4   The census returns of 1801 to 1831

The official returns

It is not the intention here to go into great detail regarding the official returns of the pre-1841 censuses, or the extant manuscript listings which were their source. Most of the former no longer exist and the latter, as locally produced drafts, do not conform to a set pattern which can be easily summarised. All that will be given in this chapter is a general outline of the type of material which was produced in the process of taking the first four censuses. Exemplars of most of the official forms described in this chapter can be found attached to the schedules of the various pre-1841 Census Acts (see Appendix 1). Some of these have been reproduced in Appendix 3.

In 1801 two printed forms were sent by John Rickman to every parish in England and Wales. The first was the 'Form of Answers by the Overseers'. This was divided into nine boxes or sections. The first four were for the county, hundred, city and town, and parish. The fifth related to houses in the parish, and was broken down into spaces for the number of inhabited houses, the number of families inhabiting them and the number of uninhabited houses. The next box was divided in two for the number of males and females in the parish, and the seventh was for the total number of persons. The penultimate box was divided into three for the totals of persons chiefly employed in the three occupational categories outlined in Chapter 2 (that is, agriculture; trade, manufactures, or handicraft; and the number not occupied in the preceding classes). The last box was for the sum of the three occupational groups which was supposed to be equal to the population of the parish shown in box number seven.

The second form was the 'Form of Answers by the Clergyman' which was divided up into columns for the insertion of data from the parish registers on the annual number of baptisms, burials and marriages. The columns for baptisms and burials had years in the margins starting in 1700, proceeding by decades until 1780, and then individual years up till 1800. The marriage column was marked off in individual years starting in 1754 through to 1800. Both forms contained spaces for comments to be made on the information in the returns, and for attestations of its accuracy.

The 1811 forms were somewhat similar. The overseer's return, however, was divided up into boxes in which he was to supply from left to right: the name and description of the parish; the number of inhabited houses; the number of families inhabiting them; the number of houses being built; the number otherwise uninhabited; the numbers of families chiefly employed in the three economic categories; and finally the numbers of males, females and all persons. The overseer was asked to comment on the possible reasons for any change since the last census in the number of persons in the parish. Similarly, the clergyman's return was only marked off into the ten years of the decade 1801 to 1810.

The 1821 returns were almost identical to those of the previous census but an additional form was sent on which the overseer was to give an account of the ages of the people in his parish. This was in two halves for males and females. Each half was divided into thirteen columns. These were headed under 5, 5 to 10, 10 to 15, 15 to 20, 20 to 30, and then in units of ten, up to 100 and upwards. At the bottom of each column was a space for column totals.

In 1831 much more complicated questions were asked, and more complicated and numerous forms distributed. The form for the overseers was divided into a series of subdivided boxes in the following manner:

Main heading		*Sub-heading*
1	Parish	
2	Number of inhabited houses	
3	Number of families occupying them	
4	Number of houses being built	
5	Number of other inhabited houses	
6	Families chiefly employed	1 in agriculture 2 in trade, manufactures and handicraft 3 in other than 1 and 2
7	Number of persons	1 males 2 females 3 total
8	Number of males twenty years and over	
9	Number of such males employed in agriculture	1 occupiers of land employing labourers 2 occupiers of land not employing labourers 3 agricultural labourers
10	Number of such males in manufacturing or making manufacturing machinery	
11	Number of such males in retailing or handicrafts	
12	Number of wholesale merchants, capitalists, bankers, professional persons and 'other educated men' over nineteen years	
13	Number of labourers over nineteen years employed by the preceding three classes	
14	Number of retired, superannuated or disabled males over nineteen years	

The form then provided spaces for the overseers to insert the following pieces of information:

1   the number of male servants under twenty years and twenty and over, and the number of female servants;
2   the occupations in which those in 10 above were employed, and the proportion in 13 above employed in quarrying, mining, fisheries or public works;
3   reasons for the differences between 1821 and 1831;
4   general remarks.

The overseers were also supplied with a 'Formula for entry of males upwards of twenty years of age, employed in retail trade, or handicraft' on which were printed 100 of the most common occupations in the retail trades and handicrafts. The enumerator was supposed to add the numbers in his parish in each occupation to this form and use this to calculate the total number in the whole economic group. The list was to be appended to the rest of the schedule.

The clergy were given a form for the number of baptisms, burials and marriages in their parish which was similar to that of 1821. They were also supplied with a complicated table of eighteen pages (one each for the years 1813 to 1830) on which they were to indicate the ages of all those persons who appeared in their burial registers (See Appendix 3). Each page was divided into four columns which were further divided into columns for males and females. The columns had ages in years down one side and these were ruled across to create rows. These created a matrix in which the clergyman was to make slashes in the boxes formed to indicate the numbers of males or females of that age who were recorded as dying in the relevant year. Under the age of six years there was more than one row for each year, due to the higher rates of infant mortality expected. Space was also allowed for information on the 'Defective registry of ages', and the numbers in the burial grounds of 'Dissenters, jews and others'.

There was an additional form on which the clergy were asked to supply information on the numbers of illegitimate males and females born in 1830, the annual number of unregistered births, marriages and deaths, and general remarks.

The returns made by the clergymen in 1831 survive in the PRO as record class HO 71.[1] The returns for each parish were sent via the local bishop to London under separate cover. The data they contained was aggregated by hundreds and the results published for each county. The records themselves are collected into bundles by hundred and boxed by county.

The local listings

As has already been mentioned, the Census Acts empowered the overseers of the poor and clergy to ask all the questions necessary to make their returns. Some overseers took advantage of this clause to record information on named individuals and families which they used to fill in the official returns. Some of these manuscript listings were considerable

---

1   1831 Census, Clergyman's Returns (PRO: HO 71).

administrative achievements. That for Liverpool in 1801, for example, covers over 14,000 dwellings.

The form of these local listings was usually based upon the official returns, especially in the case of the 1821 enumeration of ages, with the addition of the names of families or individuals.[2] Information totally unconnected with the census, however, was sometimes collected. This included notes on bastardy cases in Smalley, Derbyshire in 1801; whether people were baptised in Horton and Woodlands, Dorset in 1821; the religious persuasion of parishioners in the Dorset parishes of Marnhull and Shaftesbury St James in the same year; and the types of houses in which families lived in Liverpool in 1801.

Plainly this sort of information, as well as the nominal data collected for compiling the official returns, would have been of use for local poor law and ecclesiastical purposes. This may explain why the local listings were preserved by the overseers of the poor and the clergy who produced them. Sometimes the link between census-taking and local administration can be seen from the documents themselves. In the case of Starston, Norfolk, a nominal listing for the 1801 census is attached to a document in the same hand giving the names of women and weekly allowances out of the poor rates. The last page of the listing for Horton in Dorset in 1821 not only gives the population total but also the number of male labourers, the level of money wages, the average poor rate per acre and the level of allowances for the aged and infirm. The 1801 nominal listing from Exton, Hampshire, appears at the end of a register of baptisms and burials for the years 1780 to 1812 compiled by the local rector, and indicates the earliest date at which family names appear in the register. The inclusion in the official returns of information relating to the poor law was suggested to the home secretary on more than one occasion.[3]

Some of these listings must have been used locally for a considerable period of time. One example for Braintree in Essex appears to be the basis for the local 1821 census return but at the end it has a summary covering the period 1801 to 1841.

The intimate connection between early census-taking, poor law administration and the established church may possibly have had some adverse effect on the willingness of certain sections of the population to co-operate in the decennial enumeration. This may explain why later in the century the GRO was so anxious to maintain the confidentiality of the information supplied, a tradition which has endured to the present day.

In some areas the process of local collection was expedited by the use of standard printed forms. An 1801 example from Midgley, Yorkshire, was printed at 'Jacobs Office, Halifax', and was based upon the official return with the addition of extra space for names. The three occupational groups in the official returns (those working in agriculture; in trade, manufactures and retailing; and in other work) were replaced, however, by farmers, traders and 'gentry'. Similar forms survive from Midgley in 1811, and for the Yorkshire parishes of Elland-cum-Greetland and Hipperholme-cum-Brighouse in 1801 and 1811.

---

2   Unless otherwise stated these examples are drawn from copies held in the archives of the Cambridge Group for the History of Population and Social Structure.

3   Home Office: Domestic Correspondence, George IV and later (PRO: HO 44): HO 44/8, Item 119a, 19 July 1821, W Henderson to Viscount Sidmouth; HO 44/20, Items 509–510, 29 July 1830, John Rickman to Thomas Venables.

In Essex, printed forms based on the official returns, for dispatch to the magistrates of the division, have survived for Ardleigh and Horndon on the Hill in 1811 and 1821. These were printed in Chelmsford and bear the standard heading, 'The Population of the Parish of –– in the County of Essex'.

As one might expect the most advanced examples of privately printed forms can be found in London. Some parishes in the City of London appear to have been using printed household schedules and enumeration books from 1801 onwards. St Nicholas Acon certainly had household schedules produced by the same printer for each of the first four censuses. There appears to have been no single London-wide format, however, although all show similarities to the aggregate returns which had to be sent to Rickman. Since the various forms were produced by different printers in the differing parishes, they were probably composed locally without any overall co-ordination. One cannot be sure, however, that every parish in the City used both printed household schedules and enumeration books for the whole period.[4] By 1831 printed household schedules were being used in Hammersmith in conjunction with a printed enumerator's book. These forms may possibly have been the forerunners of the official household schedules and enumerators' books of 1841.

---

4   Census returns (Guildhall Library: MS various): MS 3260/1–3, St Sepulchre; MS 4306, St Nicholas Acon; MS 6852, St Helen; MS 7627, St Stephen and St Benet Sherehog; MS 7697, St Catherine Cree; MS 7753, St Anne's Blackfriars; MS 8935, St Benet, Paul's Wharf; MS 10, 784, All Hallows Lombard Street.

5   The structure of the enumerators' books

The aim of this chapter is to give a detailed physical description of the enumerators' books from 1841 onwards.[1] Much of the substance of the chapter can be found in the appendixes at the end of the book. Such information is of importance from an archival point of view, and helps to put the information in the books into context. The chapter is best used, therefore, for reference purposes, as and when required. For the vast majority of those who wish to use the returns, however, this information will be of comparatively limited use and they would be advised to proceed to the following chapters.

The overall structure of the records

The enumerators' books followed a set pattern, although their sizes varied according to the number of pages allowed for the insertion of information relating to houses, households and individuals. The overall structure of the books is summarised in Appendix 2.

The pagination of the enumerators' books

Although the enumerators' books were of a standard format for each census, they could contain differing numbers of pages for nominal information. Local registrars could presumably order different books to suit the size of the enumeration districts in the area under their control.

In 1841 there were four different-sized books:
> Book A of 20 nominal pages for less than 50 inhabited houses;
> Book B of 40 pages for 50–99 inhabited houses;
> Book C of 60 pages for 100–149 inhabited houses;
> Book D of 80 pages for 150 plus inhabited houses.
Each page contained twenty-five lines for entries.

The 1851 books had a completely different format. The smallest books appear to have contained only sixteen pages for nominal information, with only twenty lines to the page. There were at least six possible sizes of book, containing sixteen, twenty-four, thirty-six, forty-eight and seventy-two pages.

---

1   Examples of the enumerators' books can be found in the relevant census classes for 1841 to 1881. Examples of those for 1891 can be found in RG 27/6, Items 71, 73, 74. The RG 27 volume for 1901 is 'Wanting' but the Office of Population Censuses and Surveys has supplied the author with a copy of the first five pages of an enumeration book. These contain printed pro forma material relating to fictitious persons rather than any information on named individuals.

In 1861 the number of lines per page reverted to twenty-five. The most commonly used books now contained thirty-four or sixty-six pages, but books containing eighty-eight and 100 pages can also be found.

In 1871 and 1881 the page of twenty-five lines was retained but a new range of books was printed with the pagination increasing in multiples of eight. The smallest book contained sixteen pages for nominal data, the next twenty-four, and so on up to at least eighty pages.

Since the 1891 and 1901 returns are closed to public inspection it is difficult to speak authoritatively about their structure. Some unused examples, however, can be found amongst departmental files, and these contain forty and seventy-two pages of thirty-one lines each. This would appear to indicate that the multiple of eight was still the basis of pagination, although the number of lines per page had increased.

The increasing number of different enumeration books available over time, and the increasing number of lines per page, might reflect the increasingly wide differences between the populations of enumeration districts. As was noted in Chapter 2, many local registrars failed to revise the boundaries of enumeration districts to take account of changes in population densities.

In very general terms, the more urban the area the larger the population of the enumeration district, and the larger the book used. In rural areas, with a greater distance between houses, the population of enumeration districts was on average smaller. It must be noted, however, that there is no consistent or infallible relationship between the size of an enumeration district and the size of the book used. Many enumerators did not fill their enumeration books and the empty pages were removed. In some cases the returns were too large for the first book used, and pages from a second, or a whole new book, were tacked onto the end.

Preliminary tables

The enumerators' books contained tables in which the enumerators were expected to summarise the contents of their books, or to provide information to place their returns in context. These always included a table giving the number of persons, houses and (from 1851 onwards) households recorded on each page. This was intended to be used by the Census Office to produce preliminary calculations of the size of the population. These were published as interim reports whilst the main task of digesting the census data was undertaken. The enumerators do not appear to have filled in these tables very accurately since their totals frequently had to be checked and corrected.

The other tables usually provided information on why people were not at home, or were temporarily present. The tables for 1841, however, appear to have represented a more concerted effort to ask subsidiary questions, along the lines of earlier enumerations. This partly reflected the absence of special arrangements to deal with certain groups of people which were introduced thereafter. After 1881 these tables were replaced by others showing the number of persons, houses and households in the differing administrative areas within the enumeration district. Over time the tables became less of a supplement to the contents of the books, and more of a summary. (See Appendix 6 for the information sought in the various tables.)

The structure of the nominal pages

The pages for nominal information, which made up the bulk of the enumerators' books, were of a standard format divided into columns for the relevant information. The headings of the columns showed the type of information to be supplied in each. The page was then divided horizontally by lines, each line being for the information on a particular individual. At the bottom of each page were boxes for the total number of houses, males and females in the relevant columns. The books contained a set of instructions and an example of how to fill in the information required. Examples of these pages, with a summary of the column headings, can be found in Appendix 3. The instructions for filling in the information are discussed in detail in succeeding chapters.

The Welsh returns and special arrangements for Jewish immigrants

Special arrangements had to be made for those parts of Wales and Monmouthshire in which English was not understood.[2] A Welsh translation of the household schedule was available from 1841 onwards. The enumerators' books, however, were always to be filled out in English. From 1871 onwards the enumerators indicated each case where a Welsh schedule had been used by placing a 'W' in the first column of the book, immediately under the number of the schedule.

From 1841 to 1881 the normal enumerators' books were used in Wales and Monmouth-shire. In 1891, however, a special question on Welsh speaking was introduced which applied solely to this area. There were now two special household schedules for Wales and Monmouth, in English and Welsh, which contained an extra column for 'Language spoken'. People were to write 'English' if they only spoke English; 'Welsh' if they only spoke Welsh; and 'Both' if they spoke English and Welsh. There was also a separate enumeration book, in English, for Wales and Monmouthshire which contained this extra column. Similar arrangements were made in 1901, although children under three years of age were to be excluded from the returns relating to language.

A mock-up of the household schedule in Yiddish and German was produced for the information of the Jewish population of East London in 1891 and 1901.[3] They were to make their returns on the normal English household schedules using the mock-up as a crib.

---

2   Examples of the household schedules issued in Wales can be found in various PRO classes: 1841, no copy appears to have survived; 1851, HO 45/3579; 1861, RG 27/3, Item 4; 1871, RG 27/4, Item 10; 1881, RG 27/5, Item 10; 1891, RG 27/6, Item 68; 1901, RG 19/11. Examples of the 1891 and 1901 English language household schedules with an extra column for language spoken in Wales can be found in RG 27/6, Item 68 and RG 19/11 respectively. An example of the 1891 enumerator's book with the extra column can be found in RG 27/6, Item 73. An example of the 1871 instruction to the enumerators regarding the marking of Welsh schedules with a 'W' can be found attached to RG 10/5628, f 2, p ii. The author would like to thank Dr W T R Pryce for bringing this reference to his attention. Similar instructions for 1881 and 1891 can be found in RG 27/5, Item 35 and RG 27/6, Item 39.

3   For 1891 see RG 27/6, Item 63; for 1901 see RG 19/11.

The returns for the Islands in the British Seas

The Islands in the British Seas were the Channel Islands and the Isle of Man. They came under the GRO along with England and Wales for the purposes of census-taking. The lieutenant governor of the island appointed a superintendent to oversee the process of census-taking for a parish or island. That person in turn appointed enumerators for the enumeration districts.

The enumeration books were very similar to those used in England and Wales.[4] The main difference was that the geographical data sought at the front of each book and at the top of each page was much simpler. In 1861 the enumerators were, for example, to supply the name of the island, of the parish, and of the relevant town or village. (See Chapter 6 for the respective headings in England and Wales.) In 1841 householders only had to indicate whether or not the members of their households were born on the island of residence, as opposed to the county of residence as in the case of England and Wales.

In 1901, however, a separate household schedule and enumerator's book was produced for the Isle of Man. This had an extra column for information to be supplied on those who spoke the Manx language.

Annotations and alterations

The enumerators' books were regarded by the GRO as merely the raw material from which the Census Office produced the tabular returns in the published *Census reports*. The books were checked both locally and in London to ensure that they contained no obvious errors. The census clerks then went through each book, taking one head of information at a time, abstracting the data on tally sheets. In this process the books were altered and annotated by the local registrars and the census clerks. On the pages of the original books these marks are in different coloured inks, crayon, or pencil, from the enumerators' returns, and can easily be detected. It is rather more difficult to spot such additions, however, on monochrome microfilm.

These marks fall into four main categories: factual corrections; additional information; marks to highlight information; and ticks used to mark each piece of information to ensure that none was overlooked.

Factual corrections are quite easily detected. Sometimes households were enumerated in the wrong parish, or even in the wrong registration district, and this would be noted. On other occasions enumerators placed ages in the wrong sex column, or placed a town in the wrong county in the birthplace column. These were often noted and corrected. The addition in column totals, and in the summary table of the numbers of persons, houses and households on each page, often had to be revised.

The addition of information often takes place in the column for occupations. The Census Office abstracted occupations under certain standard headings using occupational dic-

---

4   Examples of these books for 1841 to 1881 can be found in the census classes open at the PRO. For 1891 see RG 27/6, Item 75. The 1901 books are not open to the public but a copy of the household schedule for that year can be found in RG 19/23.

tionaries specifically designed for the purpose. Thus, all weavers, spinners, piecers, and other operatives in the cotton industry were placed under the heading 'Cotton Manufacture' in the published reports. Sometimes these standard headings are written in besides the actual term used by the enumerator. In this way 'Carpenter' is added to 'Packing case maker', 'Die maker' to 'Brass stamp cutter', and so on.

Highlighting, in the form of coloured crayon, is often found in the case of the birthplaces of those born outside the county being enumerated. The clerks had to produce tables showing the counties of birth of migrants in each county. The procedure adopted was to first highlight the birthplaces of such persons in the books and then to tabulate the data.

As the clerks were abstracting the data from the enumerators' books they often ticked each piece of information to ensure that they did not miss any. Sometimes birthplaces are ticked off in the column for medical infirmities and this can cause some confusion. It is generally safe to assume that information in the latter column was given in writing.

6 The geographical structure of the returns

Introduction

Census information was collected within a geographical framework. The purpose of the census was not simply to record the number and characteristics of the population but to give such information for administratively significant areas. The enumerators' books themselves are the returns from a particular area, which in turn was part of what had usually been an administrative entity in 1841 when the original plans of division had been drawn up. The nineteenth century was, however, a period of rapid change in administrative boundaries, and a single enumeration district could come in time to contain parts of several bureaucratic entities. These had to be recorded within the body of the enumerators' books. Subsequently the books themselves were arranged physically in the topographical order in which their populations were recorded in the published *Census reports*. This was based on a breakdown into counties, and within these into hundreds, or registration districts, and then into parishes, and so on.[1] This physical arrangement has been carried over into the reference system used at the PRO for requisitioning the census records. For a glossary of the administrative areas mentioned in the returns see Appendix 4.

The enumeration district

The enumerators' districts were subdivisions of the registrars' sub-districts. These in turn were parts of the superintendent registrars' districts set up for the purpose of the civil registration of births, marriages and deaths. These enumeration districts had originally been drawn up in 1841, and descriptions of them were retained by registrars in their plans of division. The enumeration districts were as far as possible to be made up of meaningful entities, such as parishes and townships, or parts thereof.[2]

The enumeration districts were also supposed to be of a standard size. It was assumed in 1871, for example, that if the town districts contained 200 houses, and if rural districts were so arranged that an enumerator would not be required to travel more than fifteen miles, the number of houses being less than 200, the districts would not be too large. Where there were great changes in population, registrars were advised to subdivide or amalgamate the enumeration districts in order to prevent any becoming too large or too small. Since

---

1   For a breakdown of the various areas shown in the *Census reports* see the Office of Population Censuses and Surveys & General Register Office, Edinburgh, *Guide to census reports*, pp 270–273.
2   RG 27/1, p 19.

administrative boundaries were also changing, the areas covered by enumeration districts could soon become meaningless in administrative terms.[3]

Prior to 1891 the emphasis had been on retaining the boundaries of the previous censuses, in order no doubt to facilitate comparability. Many registrars failed to revise the boundaries of districts, and considerable distortions resulted. This was especially serious where enumeration districts were originally made up of parishes with detached parts, that is, where a certain portion of the parish was geographically separate and surrounded by the land of another parish. In time these anomalies might be removed by transferring the detached part to the parish in which it lay. The former area, however, might still be included in the enumeration district covering the original parent parish. The process was accelerated by the Divided Parishes Acts, especially that of 1882 (45 & 46 Vict., c. 58), which stated that detached parts should be incorporated into the parish surrounding them.

In 1891 registrars were positively encouraged to alter the areas of the enumeration districts to take account of these changes. Many registrars appear to have altered their boundaries as a result but not sufficiently to remove all anomalies.[4]

According to an internal GRO memorandum produced in preparation for the 1911 census,[5] the populations of the 1901 enumeration districts were distributed in the following manner:

Districts with populations in the range of (persons)	Number
1– 500	10,539
501–1,000	10,770
1,001–1,500	11,521
1,501–2,000	2,910
2,001–2,500	493
2,501–3,000	112
3,001–3,401+	23

This was despite the fact that in 1901 the GRO had instructed registrars that enumeration districts should not contain more than 1,500 persons.[6] Similarly, enumeration districts could contain parts of two or more administrative counties, civil parishes, urban and rural districts, and so on. In the registration district of Chester in 1901, 262 out of 814 districts contained two or more parts of various administrative divisions.[7]

It is very difficult to give general guidance on the extent to which enumeration districts changed over time. In practice each locality varied according to individual circumstances such as changes in population, the conscientiousness of local officers, and so on. In rural

3   RG 27/4, Item 2, pp 13–14.
4   RG 27/6, Item 6, pp 11–18.
5   RG 19/45, p 18.
6   RG 19/45, p 19.
7   RG 19/45, p 15.

areas with stable populations, the districts might stay the same throughout the period, but this can hardly have been the case on the outskirts of rapidly expanding towns. One might well expect there to be a marked disjunction between 1881 and 1891 because of the changing instructions to the registrars noted above.

A registrar's district would thus comprise a number of enumeration districts. Each of these would have a number to distinguish it from the others. In 1841 each enumeration district was generally numbered 1, 2, 3, and so on, within each registrar's district. The numbering in 1851 was much more complicated. In some registrars' districts the enumerators' districts were numbered as in 1841. In others, however, one finds runs of numbers such as 1A, 1B, 1C, 2, 3, 4, 5A, 5B, and so on. These might then be subsequently renumbered so that 1A became 1, 1B became 2, and so on. From 1861 onwards the straight through numbering system, 1 to x, tended to reassert itself, although subnumbering persisted in some districts. The numbering systems used, of course, abound in local idiosyncrasies.

The front pages, or front covers, of the enumerators' books were always used to describe the geography of the enumeration district. In 1841 this page carried three types of information. The first section related to the ancient administrative areas in which the enumeration district fell: the county, the parliamentary division, the hundred, wapentake, soke or liberty, the parish, the township, the city, borough, town or county corporate, the parliamentary city or borough, and the municipal unit. Not all of this information was given, of course, since some of these entities were mutually exclusive. The second section gave the name of the superintendent registrar's district, that of the registrar's district, and the number of the enumeration district. The page was completed by a description (usually fairly brief) of the enumeration district. The information in the second and third sections was supplied by the registrar, that in the first section was supplied later by clerks at the Census Office.[8]

In 1851 the front page of the enumerators' book was headed by six boxes in which the enumerator inserted information supplied by the registrar on the areas within which the district fell: the county and parliamentary division, the parliamentary city or borough, the municipality, the superintendent registrar's district, the registrar's district, and the number of the enumeration district. There then followed a much larger space for the description of the district. This was often given in terms of the streets and numbers of houses in towns, and of administrative areas covered in the countryside.

In 1861 much more simple information was required, being the names of the superintendent registrar's district and the registrar's sub-district, and the number and description of the enumeration district. This was also the standard practice in 1871 and 1881.

In 1891 and 1901 the same information was given on the front page but the description of the enumeration district was now broken down into a deliniation of its boundary, and a separate description of its contents. In 1901 the dividing line between rural districts was usually to be the centre of well-defined roads, whilst in a town the districts were to be described as being bounded on the north by the centre of such and such a street, on the east by the centre of another named road, and so on. The statement of contents was

---

supposed to give an exhaustive list of all the streets, roads, groups of houses and detached parts.

It is an indication of how comparatively little control was exercised over the local officers that strangely aberrant forms of the description of enumeration districts can be found. These include cases where maps of the district have been supplied, or where the description includes details of the local geology and wage rates.[9]

It is important not to confuse this description of the streets or houses in the enumeration district with the order in which these appear in the body of the book. The latter was left completely up to the enumerator, who was not necessarily constrained by a description which might have been set down decades before by a since deceased registrar.

Internal geographical references

As has been noted above, an enumeration book could contain parts of several administrative units. The 1841 enumerators do not appear to have been given any clear instructions as to how to handle the returns for these entities. From 1851 onwards, however, the enumerators were instructed that the returns for particular parishes, townships, hamlets, wards, villages, and so on were not to be confounded.[10] The whole of one parish, for example, had to be entered before the entries for any part of another parish were begun. At the end of the entries for such administrative areas the enumerator had to write across the page 'End of the parish (etc.) of ––'. The rest of the page was to be left blank, the returns for the next administrative area starting on the next page.

Given the complexities of local administrative boundaries, it was inevitable that enumerators and registrars would not always correctly identify administrative areas. Such lapses were sometimes spotted by the registrars or census clerks who inspected the books, and an attempt made to correct the entries.

In order to provide an easy means of reference to the geographical entities covered in the various parts of the books, each page had space at the top for information on the administrative areas covered therein. As the century drew to a close the number of such entities generally increased because of various administrative reforms. In consequence the information to be entered at the top of each page also became more complex and extensive. From 1851 onwards the enumerators were also required to show the number of schedules issued and the number of houses and persons in various administrative areas in a summary table at the beginning of the book. (See Appendix 5 for the page headings for geographical data, and Appendix 6 for information on the tables in the various enumerators' books.)

9   HO 107/1967, f 203; HO 107/1971, f 61; RG 10/112, f 19.
10   HO 45/3579.

The overall topographical arrangement of the records

The references given to the census returns are dependent upon the order in which they have been boxed. This is based, in turn, upon the order of places in the population tables in the printed parliamentary reports. The records were arranged so that the latter could act as finding aids to them.

From 1851 onwards the published reports were arranged by registration divisions, which were made up of registration counties. The latter are broken down into superintendent registrars' districts, and these into registrars' sub-districts. The returns have been boxed, numbered, and subsequently filmed in this order. The published reports were then arranged according to the places, parishes, townships, and so on, within sub-districts. The arrangement of the records at this level, however, does not necessarily correspond exactly to the geographical order shown in the published reports.

The returns for 1841, as is so often the case, were treated in a very different manner. The information was collected on the basis of superintendent registrars' districts, registrars' sub-districts and enumerators' districts. The enumerators' books were, however, subsequently rearranged into ancient counties (in alphabetical order), and then into hundreds, wapentakes, sokes and liberties, and within these into parishes. The returns from enumeration districts in particular hundreds, wapentakes, and so on, were collected together and inserted into folders. This was done so that the published information derived from the returns could be arranged by the ancient administrative divisions of the country as in previous census reports. This explains why the front of each enumerator's book described its contents in terms of the ancient territorial divisions of the country, as well as the registration divisions.

There is, however, a further complication in respect of the 1841 returns. At some point certain counties were rearranged yet again. In the cases of Lincolnshire and Kent, the records were resorted in order to place the parishes in alphabetical order. The arrangement of the records in the case of Lancashire is even more complicated. The records were numbered and filmed in this complex order. The rearrangement of the records does not, therefore, duplicate that found in the published population tables in 1841.

7 Special returns

The administration of the census from 1841 onwards was based on the assumption that people lived in relatively stable households or families. The first stage in the process of data capture was the distribution of 'householders' schedules' to each occupier, in which he or she was to record the details of the members of their household on census night. But large numbers of people were not in 'normal' households on census night and special arrangements had to be made for their enumeration. These included the inmates of institutions, the crews of vessels afloat, and the army. Special arrangements also had to be made for the enumeration of itinerants and night workers.

The population tables in the published *Census reports* often contain footnotes indicating places where the returns for institutions, ships , itinerants and other special categories occur. The early reports, especially that of 1851, contain the most detailed information.

Inmates of institutions

According to the 1840 Census Act the 'master or keeper – of every public or charitable institution which shall be determined upon by the said (census) commissioners, shall act as the enumerator of the inmates thereof'. In order to produce a list of such entities, superintendent registrars were obliged to send a return of these institutions (defined as every gaol, prison, penitentiary, house of correction, hulk or prison ship, workhouse, almshouse, hospital, infirmary, asylum, madhouse, public school, endowed school, college, barrack, and 'other public or charitable institutions') in their districts to the GRO.[1] The census commissioners then decided which institutions would be enumerated by their head officers. The superintendent registrar was provided with a list of these, which was passed down to the normal enumerators for information. The former also received special institutional enumeration books which they forwarded to the heads of the institutions.[2] The latter enumerated the inmates of their institutions and passed their books on to the Census Office in London. Institutions not subject to these special arrangements were treated as if they were households by the normal enumerators.

It is difficult to say on exactly what criteria institutions were selected for special treatment in 1841. The number of inmates does not appear to be a consistent guide, although very large and important institutions would usually be treated separately. Nor were particular

1   RG 27/1, pp 21–22.
2   RG 27/1, pp 77–78. Examples of the institutional books can be found in various PRO record classes: 1841 and 1851, 1841 and 1851 Census Returns (PRO: HO 107); 1861, RG 27/3, Item 18; 1871, RG 27/4, Item 23; 1881, RG 27/5, Item 21; 1891, RG 27/6, Item 68; 1901, RG 19/11.

types of institutions treated in a consistent manner. Some small asylums, for example, were returned in special institutional books, whilst others appear as households amongst the normal returns.

This plainly caused problems for the Census Office. Although the 1851 procedures respecting institutions were almost the same as in 1841, the superintendent registrars were now asked to return the number of inmates they contained at the beginning of the year. Institutions which had more than 200 inmates were now to be automatically treated as special cases to be returned in institutional books, although some smaller institutions were also to be enumerated in the same manner. This figure was retained for the censuses of 1861 to 1881. In 1891, however, the critical number of inmates was reduced to 100. Since the census was taken several months after the superintendent registrars made their surveys of institutions, some exceeding the critical size on census night were treated as normal households whilst others containing under that number were enumerated in the special institutional books.[3]

Although the household returns and the institutional books were forwarded to the Census Office separately, they had to be brought together to enable the calculation of population totals for each locality. The institutional books are usually associated with the areas in which they stood. In 1841 they can usually be found at the end of the household returns for the place concerned, or of the returns for the hundred in which they lay. In later years they can be found at the end of the returns for the relevant place, or for the registration district. The returns have also been microfilmed in this order.

The format of the institutional books was similar to that of the household returns. The main differences were:

1   the geographical information carried at the head of every page of the household returns only appeared on the first page of the institutional returns;
2   the columns for information on addresses and housing were omitted;
3   the column for relation to head of household was replaced by one for 'position in the institution' in 1851, and by another for 'relation to head of family or position in the institution' thereafter;
4   the preliminary tables only gave information on the number of males and females per page; and the total number of officers, members of officers' families and inmates;
5   there was, of course, no attempt to divide the population into houses or households.

From 1851 onwards the information on the residents of the institution had to be entered in a set order. First came the master or head of the institution, and then his or her spouse, children, other relatives, and servants. Then came the officers, their families and servants, visitors and so on. The inmates were then enumerated in their turn.

---

3   *1851 census report: population tables, I*, pp 1852–53 LXXXV [1631], p xii; *1861 census report*, p 1; *1871 census report*, PP 1873 LXXI Pt II [872–I], Appendix B: mode of taking the census, p 169; RG 27/5, Item 17; RG 27/6, Item 6, p 16.

The quality of information in the institutional returns varied according to the conscientiousness of the officers, and the type of inmates being enumerated. Very young children at boarding school might not know their place of birth, whilst elderly people in workhouses might not be seen as having any occupations. The returns relating to occupations are generally rather poor. It is almost impossible to reconstruct the possible relationships between inmates within institutions since only their status within the institution is given. In 1861 it is even difficult to identify inmates by name since only initials needed to be returned. On the other hand, one may assume that the information relating to medical disabilities would be more reliable in workhouses and hospitals.

The enumeration of the Army

Soldiers in barracks in England and Wales were always enumerated in the same manner as the inmates of other institutions. Small barracks were treated as private households to be enumerated by the ordinary enumerator. Barracks large enough to be treated separately were returned in institutional books, marked 'B' for barracks in 1851 and 1861 at least, by the resident barrack or quarter master. The position of barrack returns in the records is similar to that of other institutions.

Members of the British Army stationed abroad were never fully enumerated. Instead the military authorities provided the Census Office with information as to the numbers of officers, other ranks, wives and children, either by place or by regiment [4] Nominal information on this considerable body of men and women was never collected as part of the nineteenth-century censuses.

The enumeration of the Royal Navy

The enumeration of the Senior Service was more comprehensive than that of the Army. Members of the Royal Navy ashore in England and Wales on census night were always recorded in the usual household and institutional returns. From 1861 onwards the commanding officers of naval vessels, both in home waters and abroad, were furnished with special naval schedules in which they were to record the names and relevant details of their officers and crew.[5] In 1841 and 1851 some attempt appears to have been made to gather information regarding the members of the Royal Navy on board ship. In 1841 only a headcount was probably attempted but in 1851 special schedules appear to have been issued to the commanding officers of vessels in British ports.[6] Given the lack of detailed instructions or surviving ships' schedules, it is difficult to be dogmatic on the subject.

4   RG 27/1, pp 139–140; *1851 census report: population tables, I,* p xvii; *1861 census report,* pp 3–4; RG 27/4, Items 41 & 42; RG 27/5, Items 37 & 38; RG 27/6, Items 20 & 21; RG 19/19.

5   Examples of the Royal Navy ships' schedules can be found in the PRO record class RG 27: 1861, RG 27/3, Item 45; 1871, RG 27/4, Item 24; 1881, RG 27/5, Item 22; 1891, RG 27/6, Item 76. No schedule appears to have been issued in 1841. There is evidence that one was used in 1851 but no examples have survived. The 1901 census returns are closed to public inspection but the Royal Navy schedule used in 1901 was probably similar to that of 1891 (see RG 19/20, 15 Dec 1900, GRO draft letter to the Admiralty).

6   RG 27/1, pp 140–141; *1851 census report: population tables, I,* p xvii; *1851 census report: tables of the population and houses,* PP 1851 XLIII [1399], p iv.

The naval schedules of 1861 to 1881 contained columns for name and surname, rank or rating ('quality' in 1861), condition, age, and birthplace. These returns related to passengers as well as to servicemen. They also contained three tables giving an abstract of the numbers returned on each page of the book; the number of officers, men, boys and marines on board and on shore; and the number of passengers and other persons not borne on the books of the ship on board on census night. The schedules of 1891 and 1901 contained columns for name and surname, relation to vessel (member of the crew, etc.), condition as to marriage, age last birthday, profession or occupation, whether employer, employee or self-employed (for passengers only), birthplace, and medical disabilities. There were schedules containing differing numbers of pages for vessels of differing sizes.

If nominal returns were made for naval vessels in 1841 and 1851, they do not appear to have survived. In 1861 the returns for such vessels in both home and foreign waters can be found at the end of the record class, with those for the merchant marine. They do not appear to be in any particular order. Thereafter only the returns of naval vessels at sea or foreign waters were placed at the end of the record class. The schedules for those in British ports can usually be found at the end of the household returns for the registration district in which the port lay.

The enumeration of the merchant marine

Any attempt to describe the enumeration of the merchant marine in the nineteenth-century censuses must, of necessity, be a very complex business. The main reason for this is that the enumeration of the merchant marine, unlike almost every other aspect of the census, was not done on one day but was spread over a period of time. This period varied from census to census. Nor were all merchant vessels, or those on board them, treated in the same manner. These complexities confused the officers responsible for enumeration, who sometimes failed to follow their instructions properly, thus adding to the confusion. The very vagueness of some of these instructions, and the loss of some of the returns, makes a comprehensive description of the process even more difficult. The following should be regarded as a rough outline of the enumeration of the merchant marine and not an exhaustive account.

Throughout the period the crew and passengers of merchant vessels of whatever nationality who were on shore on census night were treated as normal residents and enumerated in the household returns. It could be argued that such people were not normal residents since they were in transit. But this is a rather narrow, legalistic point of view. The individuals who made up the floating population of ships' crews and passengers may not have been normally resident in specific ports but the presence of such people was a typical feature of many coastal towns. To exclude them from any analysis would give a hopelessly distorted picture of the population, society and economy of towns such as Liverpool, Southampton and London. The enumeration of the crews and passengers of merchant ships who were on board on census night is far more complex, and is best treated on a census by census basis.

In 1841 no attempt appears to have been made to make a complete enumeration of the latter population. Instead the GRO asked the General Register and Record Office of

Seamen to provide the number of seamen's names on its register on 6 June 1841, after deducting those reported dead. Only a global figure for the total number of merchant seamen was given in the *1841 census report*.[7]

This caused problems for the registrars of births, marriages and deaths in ports. The populations of their districts were calculated on the basis of the population on shore. Those registered as dying in the districts, however, were drawn from this population plus those on board ship in harbour. This meant that calculations of deaths per thousand population, the most important nineteenth-century sanitary statistic, were hopelessly inflated. This was extremely serious given the Victorian concern over the health of ports.[8] From 1851 onwards some attempt was made to capture the population of vessels in harbour. The GRO's net was spread even wider, however, to include vessels in certain categories which arrived in port within a certain period of time after census night.

The seagoing population to be enumerated in 1851 comprised three groups: **1** those who slept on board vessels in harbour on 30 March, 1851 (census night); **2** those on that night who were at sea in vessels engaged in the home trade (all vessels trading or sailing within the limits of the coasts of the United Kingdom, Jersey, Guernsey, Sark, Alderney, the Isle of Man, and of Europe from the Elbe to Brest); **3** those who were absent from the United Kingdom in ships normally sailing to and from foreign parts. The latter group, certainly those sailing to foreign parts, was not supposed to be fully enumerated, a headcount being undertaken via the General Register of Seamen. The first and second group were to be enumerated by the customs officers.[9]

The ships in harbour on census night were subdivided into two groups: **i** ships of foreign nations; **ii** British ships in the home or foreign trade. In the case of foreign vessels, the name and nation of the vessel, and the number and sex of persons on board, were returned by the customs officers, distinguishing foreign from British subjects. For the purpose of enumerating persons aboard British vessels in the home trade (but apparently not in the foreign trade), a special ships' schedule was produced for recording the names and details of the crew and passengers.[10]

On 15 March the customs officers gave a ship's schedule to the master of every British ship in port. They also gave one to the master of every British ship which arrived at the port unprovided with a schedule from that day until census day, 30 March. Early on the morning of 31 March, the customs officers collected the returns filled up by the masters of the ships in port on that day. From the surviving accounts it is not clear if this included British vessels engaged in foreign trade, as well as those in the home trade. Ships engaged in the home trade which were at sea on census night were supplied, either before their

---

7   RG 27/1, p 142; *1841 census report: abstract of the answers and returns*, p 297.

8   This was especially true with regard to the spread of venereal disease. See, for example, P McHugh, *Prostitution and Victorian social reform* (London, 1980).

9   Examples of the merchant ships' schedules can be found in various PRO classes: 1851, HO 45/3579; 1861, RG 27/3, Item 40; 1871, RG 27/4, Items 8 & 9; 1881, RG 27/5, Items 8 & 9; 1891, RG 27/6, Item 67; 1901, RG 19/11. A ships' schedule does not appear to have been produced in 1841. The instructions to the customs officers can be found in various PRO classes: 1861, RG 27/3, Item 42; 1871, RG 27/4, Item 36; 1881, RG 27/5, Item 34; 1891, RG 27/6, Item 23; 1901, RG 19/21. The instructions for 1851 do not appear to have survived.

10   *1851 census report: population tables*, I, p xvii.

departure or on their return, with ships' schedules, which were collected as the vessels arrived in British ports from 31 March to the last day of April. On the last day of April the ships' schedules collected were sent direct to the Census Office in London.

This process was plainly very complex. The intention was to restrict a nominal enumeration to the crew and passengers of British vessels engaged in the home trade, either in port on census night, or arriving within a month. It is not clear if British vessels engaged in foreign trade were so enumerated, although the wording of the schedule would indicate not. The apparent destruction of most of the ships' schedules for this census makes it difficult to settle the question. For all other vessels only a headcount was officially attempted.

The 1851 ships' schedule was, with minor changes, used throughout the nineteenth century, the only major additions being extra columns to bring the information sought into line with the household schedules. On the front of the schedule the master of the ship was to indicate the port to which the ship belonged, its name, its registration number and date of registration, its tonnage, whether it was employed in the home trade, conveying passengers or fishing, the name of the master, and the number of his master's certificate. He was also to record the date and port at which he received the schedule, the position of the ship at midnight on 30 March, 1851, and the port at which he delivered the schedule. Inside, the master was to indicate the names of the passengers and crew, the number of the master or mate's certificate, the number of the register ticket, if people were members of the crew ('C'), passengers ('P'), or visitors ('V'), their condition as to marriage, their sex ('M' or 'F'), their age last birthday, their rank, profession or occupation, their birthplace, and the usual medical disabilities. In later censuses a box was provided in which the master inserted the number of persons from the vessel on shore on census night. In 1901 their names and full census details had to be given. Information on whether the vessel was powered by steam or sails was sought from 1891.

The administrative arrangements for the enumeration of the merchant marine in 1861 can be traced with much greater certainty. A ships' schedule similar to that of 1851, and known as 'Form A', was given by the customs officers to the master of every British foreign-going, home-trade and coasting ship or vessel in port on 25 March, or which arrived between that day and census day, 7 April. These were to be collected on 8 April. On the arrival in port of any British home-trade or coasting vessel between that day and 7 May, the master was to be asked if he had handed in his census return at any UK port. If not he was requested to fill up a ship's schedule and to hand it to the customs officer. Another schedule, known as 'Form B', was used by the customs officers to record the number of persons who slept on board ships of foreign nations or British colonies on census night, distinguishing foreigners, and British subjects by sex.[11] This was done by the enumerators who went on board such ships on 8 April.

11   RG 27/3, Item 41.

These instructions should have meant that only British ships in the coasting or home trade which arrived in port within a certain period, or British ships in the foreign trade which were in port on census night, should have been issued with ships' schedules. British foreign-going ships in foreign waters before 8 April should not have been given schedules, and only a headcount should have been taken of those on foreign vessels in port on census night. An examination of the schedules, however, reveals British ships which were in the Baltic and Mediterranean on census night. These were apparently foreign-going vessels which were mistakenly given schedules by the customs officers.

The arrangements in 1871 were slightly different. In that year only ships' schedules, Form A of 1861, were used. These were to be delivered to all British and foreign vessels which arrived in port from 25 March till census day on 2 April. These were collected in port on 3 April. Further forms were only to be handed to British vessels in the coasting and home-trade which arrived in port from that day until 2 May. Thus, foreign vessels in port on census day were fully enumerated for the first time. This process was repeated in 1881, the respective periods being 26 March to 3 April, and 4 April to 3 May.

The system of enumeration changed once more in 1891. Ships' schedules were to be left aboard all vessels, whether British, foreign or colonial, which were in port on 30 March, or which arrived up till 5 April, census day. Such schedules were also to be given to every British vessel, and every foreign vessel 'employed in the coasting trade of the United Kingdom', arriving between 6 April and 30 June. This meant that the situation had been greatly simplified. All vessels in port on census day were now fully enumerated, as were all British vessels, and foreign vessels engaged in the UK coasting trade, which arrived in port in the period up to the end of June.

The instructions for 1901 were similar to those of the previous decade, the two periods now running from 23 March to 31 March, and from 1 April to 30 June. The simplicity of the 1891 arrangements was compromised, however, by the following instruction to the customs officers:

> In the cases of vessels absent from the United Kingdom on the night of the 31st of March, and on the 1st of April, but arriving before the 30th of June, Masters of Vessels may be informed that no particulars of passengers need be entered upon the shipping schedules, and that, if the vessel is foreign-going beyond the 'Home Trade' limits, particulars respecting members of the crew under an Agreement to be delivered up in the United Kingdom need not be entered upon the shipping schedule.

The position of the schedules within the census records can be summarised quite quickly. No schedules appear to have been issued in 1841. Shipping schedules were issued in 1851 but very few appear to have survived. The 1861 schedules can be found at the end of the household returns with those for the Royal Navy. In 1871 and 1881 the shipping returns are usually at the end of the household returns for the place or port to which the ships were nearest on census night, or at which they delivered their schedules. The 1891 and 1901 returns are not open to public inspection but it is probable that this arrangement continued.

Fishing vessels

Alas, further complications were introduced into the enumeration of the population at sea by the special arrangements which were made for the enumeration of fishing vessels.[12]

As with other shipping, no attempt was made to enumerate fishing vessels in 1841. The surviving accounts of the 1851 census are not detailed enough to reconstruct the position in that year. The 1851 ships' schedule, however, asked the master to state if his ship was employed in the home-trade, conveying passengers, or fishing. Fishing vessels may, therefore, have been treated in the same manner as other vessels.

In 1861 fishing vessels were to be given ships' schedules if they were in port on 4 April, or arrived between then and census day, 7 April. Whereas all British coasting and home-trade vessels arriving up till 7 May were also to be given a schedule, only fishing vessels arriving up till 20 April were to be so treated. Fishing vessels were handled in a similar manner in 1871 and 1881, except that in the period before census night they were now treated in a similar manner to other vessels. Whilst other British vessels arriving in port after census night were given ships' schedules from 3 April to 2 May in 1871, and from 4 April till 3 May in 1881, fishing vessels only received them up till 14 April and 15 April respectively.

In 1891 and 1901, however, British fishing vessels, and 'every fishing boat of foreign nationality which brings fish regularly to ports of the UK', were to be treated in the same manner as other vessels. This simplification of procedures corresponds to that for the enumeration of other vessels in this period.

The distribution amongst the household returns of the ships' schedules for fishing vessels is similar to that for other shipping.

Vessels engaged in inland navigation

In order to complete a description of the enumeration of the floating population in the nineteenth century, it only remains to consider the population of vessels engaged in inland navigation.

Such vessels which came into the areas of ports and harbours under the jurisdiction of the customs officers were treated by them in the same manner as fishing vessels. The only exception to this was in 1851, when the customs officers merely forwarded to London the vessel's name, description and port where returned, as well as the number of males and females on board.[13]

---

12   The schedules used for fishing vessels were the same as those used for other merchant ships. Examples of these schedules can be found in various PRO classes: 1851, HO 45/3579; 1861, RG 27/3, Item 40; 1871, RG 27/4, Items 8 & 9; 1881, RG 27/5, Items 8 & 9; 1891, RG 27/6, Item 67; 1901, RG 19/11. A ships' schedule does not appear to have been produced in 1841. The instructions to the customs officers respecting fishing vessels can be found in various PRO classes: 1861, RG 27/3, Item 42; 1871, RG 27/4, Item 36; 1881, RG 27/5, Item 34; 1891, RG 27/6, Item 23; 1901, RG 19/21. The instructions from 1851 do not appear to have survived.

13   *1851 census reports: population tables, I*, p xvii.

The population of such vessels on canals and inland navigable waters was treated in a rather different manner. No attempt appears to have been made to make a nominal enumeration of these vessels in 1841 and 1851. Enumerators were merely asked to calculate the numbers of males and females on such vessels and insert this figure in one of their preliminary tables. In 1841 application was also made to the canal companies to provide an estimate of the number of such people.[14]

From 1861 onwards some attempt was made to enumerate this floating population, and a calculation of the number of such persons was no longer supplied by the enumerators. The arrangements for 1861 were extremely ad hoc. The registrar was to enumerate vessels within his sub-district 'according to the circumstances of each case'. He was advised to find where such vessels might be moored from the owners or managers of wharfs, or the canal companies, and then to employ a 'trustworthy person' to visit them on census morning to obtain the necessary nominal information using the standard ships' schedule of that year.[15] These returns can now be found at the end of the household returns for the enumeration district, or registration sub-district, in which the vessel lay on census night.

From 1871 onwards it became the responsibility of the enumerators to enumerate such vessels.[16] They handed the persons in charge of the vessels a ship's schedule, and collected them when completed. The information they contained was then entered into their enumerator's books at the end of the household entries. From 1881 this applied not only to vessels which had been given schedules prior to census day but also to barges and the like which appeared in the enumeration district on that day.

Itinerants and travellers

Institutions and waterborne vessels created special problems for census takers but they could be easily traced and treated as if they were households. People travelling, especially those 'on the tramp', were a potentially greater problem because they were much less easy to track down. They slipped through the census net because they were not resident as part of a household on census night. In the nineteenth century many people moved about the country looking for work according to the seasons or the social calendar. The censuses of this period were usually taken in March or early April, in order to avoid the movements of population associated with the agricultural harvest. In many areas, however, there may have been itinerants sleeping rough at census time.

In 1841 no special arrangements appear to have been made to include the itinerant population in the nominal returns. This was a serious omission since the census of that year was taken in June when the movement of itinerants during the summer was already under way. The enumerators were instructed to insert in one of their summary tables the number of persons sleeping in barns, sheds, tents or in the open air, 'or who from any

14   RG 27/1, pp 81–82.
15   RG 27/3, Item 12.
16   See the instruction books circulated to the registrars and enumerators prior to census day: 1841, RG 27/1, pp 18–35; 1851, HO 45/3579; 1861, RG 27/3, Items 11–14; 1871, RG 27/4, Item 29; 1881, RG 27/5, Item 27; 1891, RG 27/6, Item 6. At the time that these records were transferred to the PRO, the volume in this series for 1901 was recorded as being 'Wanting'. The instructions for the officers taking the 1901 census in the Islands in the British Seas (the Isle of Man and the Channel Islands) can be found in RG 19/23.

other cause, although within the district, have not been enumerated as inmates of any dwelling-house'.[17] In order to get some idea of the numbers travelling at night by railway, canal and coach, inquiries were made with the railway and canal companies, and with 'Mr Horne of the Golden Cross, Charing Cross'.[18] There is, however, at least one entry for railway passengers but these appear to have been people on a train waiting in Southampton railway station, who were enumerated along with the railway employees at the station.[19]

In 1851 those sleeping in barns, sheds, tents and in the open air, were treated as in the previous census. The enumerators were instructed that persons travelling by railway or coach were to be returned at the house or hotel at which they stopped, or took up their residence, on the morning after census night, although the wording to this effect was not very clear on the household schedules. This became the standard instruction to enumerators and householders for the rest of the century.[20]

In 1861 the number of those in barns, sheds, tents and in the open air, was no longer explicitly given in one of the preliminary tables. On the other hand, as full particulars as possible of such people were now to be given in the main body of the returns. This information was to be given at the end of the household schedules under a heading 'List of persons not in houses'.[21]

From 1871 onwards particulars regarding such persons were to be entered in their proper place in the roads, lanes or outhouses in which they slept. Such barns, sheds, tents and so on were not, however, to be reckoned as houses.[22]

Nightworkers

The census was based upon the principle that the householder should record the people who slept in his or her house on census night. In 1841, however, no special arrangements appear to have been made for those away from home on nightshifts. In theory they should not have been included in the census, although householders may have done so in many cases. The enumerators, however, were asked to estimate in their tables the numbers of such people down pits and mines.[23] From 1851 onwards, however, nightworkers were to be enumerated in their homes if they returned there the next day.[24]

---

17   RG 27/1, p 46.
18   RG 27/1, pp 81–82.
19   HO 107/417, bk 7, f 9.
20   HO 45/3579.
21   RG 27/3, Item 17, p i.
22   Examples of the enumerators' books can be found in the relevant census classes for 1841 to 1881. Examples of those for 1891 can be found in RG 27/6, Items 71, 73, 74. The RG 27 volume for 1901 is 'Wanting' but the Office of Population Censuses and Surveys has supplied the author with a copy of the first five pages of an enumeration book. These contain printed pro forma material relating to fictitious persons rather than any information on named individuals.
23   RG 27/1, p 46.
24   See the instruction books circulated to the registrars and enumerators prior to census day; 1841, RG 27/1, pp 18–35; 1851, HO 45/3579; 1861, RG 27/3, Items 11–14; 1871, RG 27/4, Item 29; 1881, RG 27/5, Item 27; 1891, RG 27/6, Item 6. At the time that these records were transferred to the PRO, the volume in this series for 1901 was recorded as being 'Wanting'. The instructions for the officers taking the 1901 census in the Islands in the British Seas (the Isle of Man and the Channel Islands) can be found in RG 19/23.

Part III   The interpretation of census data

8   Information relating to houses

The information in the census returns relating to housing is important for several reasons. For the family historian the address of a house is usually the means by which he or she locates an ancestor. For the historian of housing the ratio of people to houses, the amount of unoccupied property, and the number of families in tenements with under five rooms, are important indications of the state of the housing market, and of the degree of overcrowding. For the social and economic historian the layout of streets, their social composition, the extent to which differing social classes lived next to each other, are all significant matters.

Unfortunately, the data relating to housing in the census can be extremely difficult to interpret, especially in heavily built-up areas. What exactly constituted a 'house', what made one 'uninhabited', and what was a 'room', were never adequately defined in the period. Nor were addresses necessarily stable entities. Some of these problems will be outlined here in general terms. The practice of different enumerators and local conventions could differ widely, however, and these need to be considered individually in any local study.

Information relating to 'houses' in the census returns

At first sight the information relating to houses appears fairly unambiguous. (The descriptions given here should be used in conjunction with the examples of pages from the enumerators' books shown in Appendix 3.) In 1841 the 'Place' column contained the names of houses, streets, or places, but not necessarily the numbers of houses. The column headed 'Houses' was divided into two columns; for uninhabited houses or those being built, and inhabited houses. The beginning of an inhabited house was marked by the enumerator with a number 1 in the latter column, adjacent to the name of the first person in the house. The end of the house was to be marked by double oblique strokes (//) inserted after the name of the last person in the house on the line dividing the houses and names columns. An uninhabited house or one being built, was to be recorded by placing '1 U' or '1 B' respectively in the relevant division of the houses column, by the names of the people in the inhabited house nearest to which it stood.

In 1851 the enumerator was expected to record the name of the street, place or road, and the name or number of the house in the second column of the schedule. Under the last name of any house he was to draw a line across the page from left to right as far as the fifth column. Where there was an uninhabited house or one being built to be recorded, this was done by writing in the address column on the line under the last name in the last inhabited house, 'one house uninhabited', 'three houses building', and so on. A line was then drawn under this in the same manner as for inhabited houses.

In 1861 the address column was similar to that of the previous census. The houses column of 1841 was, however, reintroduced. The beginning of an inhabited house was marked by the enumerator with a number 1 in the relevant column, adjacent to the name of the first person in the house. The end of the house was to be marked by double oblique strokes (//) inserted after the name of the last person in the house on the line dividing the houses and names columns. An uninhabited house or one being built, was to be recorded by placing '1 U' or '1 B' respectively in the relevant division of the houses column, immediately below the name of the last person in the adjacent inhabited house. The entries of the next house were to start immediately underneath. The addresses of such houses were also to be inserted.

This layout was to be repeated in 1871, 1881 and 1891, although the double oblique strokes now ran in the opposite direction (\\). In the latter year, however, a new column was added for the number of rooms occupied by each family in the house, if under five. This number was to be supplied next to the name of the head of the household.

In 1901 the houses column was broken down into four divisions; inhabited houses, uninhabited houses which were usually in occupation, uninhabited houses which were not usually in occupation, and those which were being built. The enumerator was now only expected to place a number 1 in the relevant column. The question as to the number of rooms inhabited was repeated.

In all the censuses the enumerators were expected to total the numbers of each type of house on the page, and to give this information at the foot of each house column.

These apparent certainties begin to dissolve, however, as one explores the meaning of the terms used.

The definition of a house

In a rural setting, or the middle-class suburbs of large towns, the identification of a house or cottage might be fairly simple. But in the 'rookeries' of the great cities, where older buildings had been subdivided and rooms partitioned to squeeze in the ever increasing urban population, there were insuperable problems. Buildings frequently clustered behind and in part on top of others, two front doors might serve the same block, and one flat sometimes went over the top or through into part of a neighbouring building. Much the same could be said of cellar dwellings which existed in some mid-century towns. There were also constant problems with outbuildings which might, or might not, be occupied, with or without the knowledge of their owners.

The 1841 instructions to the enumerators were not particularly helpful:

> By "House" is meant *Dwelling-House*; and every building in which any person habitually sleeps must be considered as a dwelling-house.[1]

1   1841 and 1851 Census Returns (PRO: HO 107).

But what of buildings which provided temporary shelter for a person on census night, and how did one define a 'building'?

From 1851 onwards the house was defined as the space between the external and party walls of a building.[2] This was as much a legal as a physical description since a party wall was one between two buildings or pieces of land intended for distinct occupation, in the use of which each of the occupiers had a partial right. The definition depended in part, therefore, on finding an 'occupier'. In the maze of dark back-alleys and courts in London and the industrial cities, it may have been difficult for enumerators to make such an identification.

This definition of the house created anomalies in the late nineteenth century with the erection of model or industrial dwellings for the working classes, the precursors of modern high-rise blocks. Each block was officially treated as a single but subdivided house, although each flat was a self-contained dwelling unit. In Scotland, where such buildings had been common from a much earlier date, the definition of a house had long since included that of a dwelling with a door opening directly onto common stairs. To complicate matters still further some enumerators, following common sense but not their instructions, chose to regard every such flat as a separate house.[3]

The introduction in 1891 of the question on the number of rooms occupied by each household appears to have made the situation worse. This entity was termed a 'tenement' by the GRO. Many enumerators appear to have assumed that a tenement and a house were the same thing, and the house became the space occupied by a single household.[4] The household was also in turn a difficult entity to define. (See Chapter 9.)

What was included and excluded from the definition of a house varied from census to census.[5] In 1841 buildings such as churches or warehouses, 'which were never used or intended to be used as dwelling-houses', were not to be counted as houses. On the other hand the enumerator was given the rather garbled instruction that,

2   See the instruction books circulated to the registrars and enumerators prior to census day: 1841, RG 27/1, pp 18–35; 1851, HO 45/3579; 1861, RG 27/3, Items 11–14; 1871, RG 27/4, Item 29; 1881, RG 27/5, Item 27; 1891, RG 27/6, Item 6. At the time that these records were transferred to the PRO, the volume in this series for 1901 was recorded as being 'Wanting'. The instructions for the officers taking the 1901 census in the Islands in the British Seas (the Isle of Man and the Channel Islands) can be found in RG 19/23.
3   *1891 preliminary census report*, PP 1890 XCIV [c. 6422], p vi; *1890 report of the Treasury Committee on the Census*, PP 1890 LVIII [c. 6071], QQ 1734–1736; RG 19/45, f 49.
4   *1891 census report*, PP 1893–94 CVI [c. 7222], p 20.
5   See the instruction books circulated to the registrars and enumerators prior to census day: 1841, RG 27/1, pp 18–35; 1851, HO 45/3579; 1861, RG 27/3, Items 11–14; 1871, RG 27/4, Item 29; 1881, RG 27/5, Item 27; 1891, RG 27/6, Item 6. At the time that these records were transferred to the PRO, the volume in this series for 1901 was recorded as being 'Wanting'. The instructions for the officers taking the 1901 census in the Islands in the British Seas (the Isle of Man and the Channel Islands) can be found in RG 19/23. Examples of the enumerators' books can be found in the relevant census classes for 1841 to 1881. Examples of those for 1891 can be found in RG 27/6, Items 71, 73, 74. The RG 27 volume for 1901 is 'Wanting' but the Office of Population Censuses and Surveys has supplied the author with a copy of the first five pages of an enumeration book. These contain printed pro forma material relating to fictitious persons rather than any information on named individuals. RG 27/1, p 70.

In the case of a house having a stable or outhouse belonging to it, in or over which some person of the household sleeps, the enumerator must take care that such person is neither inserted as an inmate of such other detached building in which he sleeps, which must be entered as a separate dwelling house.

This could be taken to mean that a stable slept in by a groom was to be counted as a separate house.

In 1861 the enumerators were told to ignore the 'out-offices attached to a mansion', and the outbuildings of farms. But a stable or coach-house, if a detached building containing dwelling rooms, was to be regarded as an inhabited house. This applied presumably even if the 'dwelling room' was a mattress in the corner of the stable on which a young groom slept. In 1901 it was pointed out that blacksmiths' forges, workshops, and stables, without sleeping accommodation, should not be treated as houses.

The carelessness of the enumerators when filling out their books also creates difficulties. Occasionally long lines or double slashes defining a house have been accidently omitted, whilst on other occasions short lines and single slashes defining a household were drawn in error as long lines and double slashes. These errors can often be spotted by changes of address, or by consulting the totals for the numbers of houses at the bottom of each page. But even this may fail where the address information is minimal or confused.

The census authorities were fully aware of these problems and admitted privately that in many urban areas the numbers of houses shown in the enumerators' books and reproduced in the census reports were 'misleading and often valueless'. They also felt that in the absence of any indication of the size of houses, it was dangerous to use the changing numbers of houses from census to census as part of an index of overcrowding.[6]

If census material is to be used to study urban housing conditions, it must be treated with great caution. If addresses, rate books, maps and street directories exist, these should be consulted to identify possible problems of misenumeration. In many cases, however, this will not be possible. In such circumstances, the double oblique stroke and the '1' in the inhabited houses column, or the long line in 1851, may have to be accepted as indicating the existence of a new house. It should be recognised, however, that such 'houses' may not necessarily be particularly meaningful entities in urban areas.

The only exceptions which seem useful to allow are the following:[7]

1   Where '1' or the long line is placed in the middle of a nuclear family (as indicated in the 'relationship to head of family' column and by a similar surname), and where the entry for the 'head' of this family is not preceded by a '1' or a long line, the marks may be assumed to be misplaced and suitable adjustments may be made to correspond with the sense. If this is not done members of the same family will appear to be living in the same household, but in different houses, which is plainly nonsensical.

6   RG 19/45, f 50; *1901 census report*, PP 1904 CVIII [Cd. 2174], p 37.
7   These are based on M Anderson, 'Standard tabulation procedures for the census enumerators' books 1851–1891', in *Nineteenth-century society*, ed. Wrigley, pp 139–140.

2   Long lines and double strokes are occasionally omitted at the bottom of pages. Where it is suspected that this has occurred, reference should be made to the total of inhabited houses at the foot of the next page and, where this total can only be correct if the first household on the page did indeed occupy a separate house, this may be taken as a substitute indicator, and a new house counted.

3   It may occasionally happen that a long line or double strokes are followed (from 1851) by the term 'lodger'. This should normally be taken to indicate a house where the head was absent so that the lodger should be taken as a 'head equivalent'. This conclusion should always be verified against the total at the foot of the page, and against the address when given.

4   Some enumerators occasionally omit the entry '1' in the inhabited house column in cases where they indicate a new house by a double stroke, and by a new and different address in the address column. In such cases it should be assumed that the '1' has been omitted. Unfortunately enumerators frequently omitted addresses and so they cannot be used as a general indicator.

The definition of uninhabited houses and those being built

The ratio of empty houses, or those being built, to occupied houses in the census books and reports has been used to give an indication of 'spare capacity' in the housing market.[8] There are problems, however, in accepting such calculations uncritically. These stem from the definition of a 'house', the use of the term 'uninhabited', and the fact that the census was a snapshot of the housing market on one particular day every ten years.

The census 'house' was defined, at least from 1851 onwards, in terms of the space of a building between party walls. Except in 1841, the house was not specifically defined as a 'dwelling-house' in which people lived. It could presumably be interpreted as a lock-up office, shop, or warehouse. An 'uninhabited house' might, therefore, be a building which was never inhabited, as opposed to one which was temporarily vacant. In the course of the nineteenth century such buildings became more common, especially in the commercial centres of towns. An increasing ratio of uninhabited to inhabited houses does not necessarily mean increased 'spare capacity' in the market for human habitations. Many uninhabited dwelling-houses might not be available in the housing market, because they were only empty on census night while families were away visiting. These problems led the census authorities in 1901 to make a distinction between uninhabited houses in occupation for business or other purposes, and those not in occupation for any purpose, although they admitted that the distinction appeared to have been lost on enumerators and householders. Any calculations of the ratios of empty to inhabited houses must be treated with caution.

Much the same could be said about houses being built. A declining ratio of houses being built to those completed on census night has little meaning unless one can assume that the time needed to complete houses remained constant throughout the nineteenth century. If

8   B R Bristow, 'Population and housing in nineteenth-century urban Lancashire: a framework for investigation', *Local Population Studies*, XXXIV (1985), pp 12–26. The author is plainly aware of the problems of using the census data relating to housing.

builders could put up houses more quickly because of changing techniques, then on any one day there would need to be fewer houses in the process of being built to maintain the building/built ratio over the whole year. The speed of building might also vary, of course, from region to region.

Nor does the number of houses being built on one day in every tenth year necessarily indicate the state of the construction industry over long periods. The figures in any census year might indicate quite temporary conditions. In 1891, for example, it was believed that the low number of houses being built was due to the severe and prolonged frost in the early months of the year.[9]

Even where the definition of the house is unambiguous, the number of people resident in it, as shown in the census, may not be an exact measurement of the degree of overcrowding. In some areas where nightshifts were common, one group of people might occupy the house by day and another set by night. But because of the conventions used to record nightworkers both groups would appear together as residents of the same house.

All such calculations need to be treated with extreme caution, and with due regard to changing local conditions, temporary aberrations, and changes in building techniques. They also depend upon the assumption that the 'house' itself is a meaningful entity.

Addresses in the census

The addresses of houses are of fundamental importance for family historians tracing their ancestors, or social historians attempting to reconstruct residential patterns and mobility rates. The nineteenth century was, however, a period of rapid urban expansion, and of a revolution in postal services. These had a profound effect on the system of addresses used nationally, and create problems for modern researchers.

The enumerators were given very clear instructions with regard to the provision of address data. In 1841 it was only necessary for the enumerator to give the name, if any, of the house, or the name of the street, or part of the town, village, or hamlet in which it stood. From 1851 onwards, however, they were specifically instructed to give the number of the house as well.[10]

This depended, however, on the existence of proper addresses in the first place. The rapid expansion of towns and the subdivision of houses in the early nineteenth century had left addresses in chaos. The Towns Improvement Clauses Act of 1847 provided that local authorities should from time to time renumber houses and buildings, and this requirement was incorporated into the 1875 Public Health Act. Street numbering systems, therefore, did not become formalised in many towns until the 1850s at the earliest. Liverpool, for example, renumbered on a uniform basis in 1856, with the painting and

---

9   *1901 census report*, p 36.
10   Examples of the enumerators' books can be found in the relevant census classes for 1841 to 1881. Examples of those of 1891 can be found in RG 27/6, Items 71, 73, 74. The RG 27 volume for 1901 is 'Wanting' but the Office of Population Censuses and Surveys has supplied the author with a copy of the first five pages of an enumeration book. These contain printed pro forma material relating to fictitious persons rather than any information on named individuals.

affixing of 40,538 new numbers.[11] But even as late as the 1881 census, the GRO was still haranguing the chairmen of urban sanitary authorities on the need for standard numbering systems.[12] Street numbering was often chaotic well into the nineteenth century.

This was especially serious in slum districts with courts leading off main streets, cellar dwellings, and subdivided houses. The boundaries of enumeration districts often cut across streets and this adds further complications. An additional problem may be the 'loss' of numbers in a street due to the demolition of houses for a railway station, or public works. Similarly, on the outskirts of nineteenth-century towns, at times of urban expansion, new houses were constantly being added to the ends of streets. An address found in a document postdating the census by only a few years might not have existed at the time of the decennial enumeration. The opposite problem can be encountered where whole areas of cities were swept away for major works, such as slum clearances.

The introduction of the straight-through numbering of streets could cause its own problems. In the nineteenth century housebuilding was usually in the hands of small speculative builders. Easy access to loans, and the convention of subcontracting in the building trades, meant that such builders needed neither direct employees nor capital of their own. Houses tended to be put up in small numbers by adding a run of perhaps five or six to the end of an existing street.[13] Each of these speculations could be given a separate name, Such-and-Such Terrace, Such-and-Such Place, and so on; each block having its own numbers starting from '1'. Streets could be subdivided into a series of such runs of numbers. In time these streets might be renumbered, so that the addresses ran consecutively throughout their length. This process was going on in London in the 1860s and 1870s. Addresses may not, therefore, be stable over time.

In the countryside the names of outlying farms or prominent residences will almost certainly be stated, but difficulties begin to arise when trying to identify the houses along main streets of villages, or in the populous and unnumbered streets of small towns. In country districts there may rarely have been a street number to give, and a considerable collection of dwellings may take the name of the principal house in the area.

The majority of addresses can be found in the returns with a little effort, and street indexes exist in many record offices for this purpose. In some urban areas, however, one may need recourse to contemporary maps, rate books, and commercial and postal directories to locate families and houses. This assumes, of course, that houses were put down in the returns in the order in which they appeared on the ground. In rural areas it may be necessary to go through a whole parish to find a particular family.

11   R Lawton, 'Census data for urban areas', in *The census and social structure*, ed. Lawton, p 129.
12   RG 27/5, Item 39.
13   H J Dyos, *Victorian suburb. A study of the growth of Camberwell* (Leicester, 1977), pp 122–137.

The census and studies of residential proximity

An interesting use to which the census books have been put has been the study of class segregation in cities.[14] This is done by comparing the social status of people who lived next to each other. What proportion of the middle classes lived next to members of the working classes, and how did this figure change over time? In most cases the proximity of households can be checked by comparing addresses but in areas where house numbers are not given, such studies depend upon the enumerators having entered houses in their books in the order in which they appeared in the streets.

It should be noted, however, that the enumerators were never explicitly instructed to enter the household returns in this order. From the point of view of the census authorities it was important that the houses in a particular administrative area should be grouped together for abstraction but for most purposes it did not really matter in what order the houses appeared within this area. In practice such an order was only implicit in the instructions given to the enumerators. The examples of how to fill out their book always showed the houses enumerated in the order they appeared in the streets. At the same time they were instructed that uninhabited houses, and those being built, should appear in the order in which they were to be found in the street.[15] This enforced a similar order upon the inhabited houses.

Nor were enumerators explicitly instructed to follow the description of the district on the front of their books. They were instructed to work out their own routes, and were not constrained by wording which may have been set down twenty or thirty years before. Nor does the order of the returns in the books necessarily reflect the way in which the enumerators collected them. They could collect the returns in the manner which suited them and rearrange them at home for entering in their books. One should not confuse the process of collecting the household schedules, and that of copying them into enumeration books.

The vast majority of returns do indeed follow streets and may even reflect the way in which the enumerators collected the schedules but there are examples where this does not hold true. In Ramsgate in 1851 the houses in one enumeration district are all in order within streets but the latter are not arranged topographically. The enumerator presumably bundled his schedules under street headings, and wrote these into his book at random. In the harbour area of the town at the same date, one enumerator listed all the inns first, taking them out of the order in which they appeared in the streets.[16] There may even be cases, where there were no uninhabited houses or houses being built to constrict their freedom of action, where enumerators had houses in no topographical order at all.

---

14   J Foster, *Class struggle and the Industrial Revolution: early industrial capitalism in three English towns* (London, 1974), pp 125–131.

15   See the instructions books circulated to the registrars and enumerators prior to census day: 1841, RG 27/1, pp 18–35; 1851, HO 45/3579; 1861, RG 27/3, Items 11–14; 1871, RG 27/4, Item 29; 1881, RG 27/5, Item 27; 1891, RG 27/6, Item 6. At the time that these records were transferred to the PRO, the volume in this series for 1901 was recorded as being 'Wanting'. The instructions for the officers taking the 1901 census in the Islands in the British Seas (the Isle of Man and the Channel Islands) can be found in RG 19/23.

16   R S Holmes, 'Identifying nineteenth-century properties', AREA, VI (1974), pp 276–277.

Where address data is given these problems can easily be spotted. In cases where this is vague or confused, one can compare the position of named inns and public houses in the census returns and on maps to check consistency. If this is not possible the returns should be used with considerable caution. It is always advisable to study the conventions employed by individual enumerators before embarking on such exercises.

Even when houses are arranged in a topographical sequence one must not assume that households which appear immediately adjacent to each other in the enumeration books are 'next-door neighbours'. In country areas there may be large distances between houses. In the towns the social composition of the residents of street frontages may be very different from that of the courts behind. In the enumerators' books the last house in the street frontage and the first in the court may appear adjacent to each other but on the ground they would be separated by an alleyway marking a spatial and social boundary. In such cases the consultation of contemporary maps is again of great importance.

The number of rooms in tenements

The information sought in 1891 and 1901 on the number of rooms inhabited by a family is extremely important for the historian of housing but is also extremely problematical. The householder was responsible for providing this information in 1891 but this became the enumerator's job in 1901.[17]

The place on the schedule in which the return had to be made was not very conspicuous and was limited to families occupying less than five rooms. This led to incomplete returns and undoubtedly to omissions, particularly in the case of flats and maisonettes.[18]

Nor did the Census Acts or the instructions to the householders or enumerators ever define a 'room'. Should sculleries, pantries, washrooms, landings, lobbies, closets, shops, offices, or stores, be included or not? In the case of caretakers in warehouses, offices, banks, and so on, should the number of rooms be restricted to the number of rooms in which the person or family resided?[19] This was compounded by the difficulty of defining a 'family' or 'household'. Such difficulties were never resolved in this period. Even as late as the 1981 census, a post-enumeration survey revealed that in the case of 28.6% of households the number of rooms inhabited had been given incorrectly. One might expect an equivalent or higher level of misenumeration in nineteenth-century censuses.[20]

Presumably these problems would have been fairly consistent over time, and the comparison of large areas from census to census is probably justified. But the figures should be used with great caution when comparing individual or small numbers of households in time and space.

---

17   See the household schedules for 1891 and 1901; RG 27/6, Item 68 and RG 19/11 respectively.
18   RG 19/45, f 28a.
19   RG 19/45, f 28b.
20   F Whitehead, 'The GRO use of social surveys', *Population Trends*, XLVIII (1987), pp 46–47.

9   Information relating to households

Introduction

In the manuscript censuses the people found within a house, however that was defined, could be further divided into 'families' or 'households'. In many areas, especially in the countryside, one might expect to find one socially meaningful group of people per house. In cities, however, more than one biological family, or socially linked group of individuals, could occupy a house. For social and economic historians, and historical demographers, the household or family in the census returns is of considerable importance. The study of household structure gives an insight into the workings of the nineteenth-century family, an institution of unrivalled importance in the reproduction of the population and social mores.

It should be noted, however, that the household in the census is an administrative artefact. It does not correspond to the biological family, or to the sum total of relationships between kin and other members of society. The household in census terms was those people present in a house on census night which a householder placed on his or her household schedule. Those absent from home for any length of time should not have appeared on this return, although the temptation to enter members of the household normally resident may have been strong. Sons and daughters who had grown up and left home should not have appeared in a household, nor of course would those yet to be born. Lastly, the rigorous demarcation of the population into households in the census may lead one to overlook the importance of relationships between households (especially between women), the role of kin living nearby, and support given by friends and workmates. The temptation to see Victorian society as constructed solely from the building blocks of census families should be resisted.

This has led historical demographers to refer to the census households as 'co-residing groups', rather than families. In this chapter the term 'household' is used in this specific sense to designate the grouping of individuals by administrative convention in the process of census-taking. This entity, however, may well have had considerable social meaning, especially since relationship to head was always couched in terms of the relationship to the head of 'the family'.[1]

---

1   See the examples of the household schedules which can be found in various PRO record classes: 1841, RG 27/1, pp 56–57; 1851, HO 45/3579; 1861, RG 27/3, Item 2; 1871, RG 27/4, Item 5; 1881, RG 27/5, Item 5; 1891, RG 27/6, Item 68; 1901, RG 19/11.

A more immediate problem is how to define the boundaries of such households. Essentially, how did the enumerators recognise a 'householder' to whom they should give a household schedule? Nineteenth-century households tended to be far more complex than those of today, with more living-in relatives, lodgers and servants. Should these people be included in the 'household'? Are the census households groups of people who interacted in a socially meaningful manner? These are extremely complicated issues, and one should not be surprised that they caused confusion at the time.

The household on the page

Leaving aside, for the moment, the definition of a census 'household', it is usually quite easy to spot those groups of people designated as such on the pages of the manuscript books.[2]

In 1841 the beginning of the first 'family' coincided logically with the beginning of the house but its end was signified by a single oblique stroke on the dividing line between the houses and names columns. The next 'family' then began, ending with a single stroke unless it happened to be the last household in the house. The end of a house was marked, of course, with a double stroke.

In 1851 the end of the 'family' was marked by a line across the page, similar to that indicating the end of a house, but only running across part of the second column, as well as the third and fourth. The line for the end of the house ran completely across the first four columns. In addition, the beginning of a new household was marked by a new schedule number in the column provided for that purpose.

The conventions in the later censuses were a mixture of those of 1841 and 1851. From 1861 onwards the oblique slash was used in the same manner as 1841 but the beginning of each household was also marked by a new schedule number. In 1841 the oblique slash ran from left to right but this was reversed from 1871 onwards. The 'short line' was only used in 1851.

The definition of the household

The census household comprised those persons whom an 'Occupier' put down on his or her household schedule. But how was the enumerator to identify such a person, and how were they in turn expected to define the members of their 'family'?[3]

---

2   See the examples in Appendix 3.
3   The following account is based on the examples of the household schedules which can be found in various PRO record classes: 1841, RG 27/1, pp 56–57; 1851, HO 45/3579; 1861, RG 27/3, Item 2; 1871, RG 27/4, Item 5; 1881, RG 27/5, Item 5; 1891, RG 27/6, Item 68; 1901, RG 19/11. See also the instruction books circulated to the registrars and enumerators prior to census day: 1841, RG 27/1, pp 18–35; 1851, HO 45/3579; 1861, RG 27/3, Items 11–14; 1871, RG 27/4, Item 29; 1881, RG 27/5, Item 27; 1891, RG 27/6, Item 6. At the time that these records were transferred to the PRO, the volume in this series for 1901 was recorded as being 'Wanting'. The instructions for the officers taking the 1901 census in the Islands in the British Seas (the Isle of Man and the Channel Islands) can be found in RG 19/23. See also the examples of the enumerators' books which can be found in the relevant census classes for 1841 to 1881. Examples of those for 1891 can be found in RG 27/6, Items 71, 73, 74. The RG 27 volume for 1901 is 'Wanting' but the Office of Population Censuses and Surveys has supplied the author with a copy of the first five pages of an enumeration book. These contain printed pro forma material regarding fictitious persons rather than any information on named individuals.

In 1841 instructions on this matter were really quite minimal. The enumerator

> must cause a householder's schedule paper to be left at every house in his district for the occupier, and where a floor or room is let separately, a separate paper for each occupier of every such floor or room ...

The definition of the household depended, therefore, on the position of the occupier as the person who paid rent. It is not clear, however, how someone subletting from the occupier was treated, although they should presumably have been treated as part of the occupier's 'family'. Given the absence of a column for relationship to the head of the household in 1841, it is difficult to reconstruct the treatment of lodgers.

In 1851 the enumerator was instructed to leave a separate schedule with each occupier,

> understanding by "occupier" either the resident owner or any person who pays rent, whether (as a tenant) for the whole of a house, or (as a lodger) for any distinct floor or apartment.

The intention here was plainly to define the household in terms of the occupation of a distinct space within a house. But what about those cases in which lodgers did not occupy a 'distinct floor or apartment', sharing part of the house with their landlords, or those from whom they sublet? The examples of how to fill in the schedules given to the householders and enumerators did not help to answer this question. These did not show anyone whose relationship to the head of the household was that of lodger or boarder, the households being made up of people related by kinship and marriage, servants and apprentices.

The 1851 definition of the occupier was repeated in 1861 but an attempt was made to introduce a distinction between the differing types of lodger noted above. The enumerators were now instructed that the following were amongst the cases in which one household schedule should be left:

> for a family consisting of a man, his wife, and children; or of parents, children, servants and visitors;
> for a family consisting of parents and children, *with boarders at the same table*, and the servants of the family, if any;
> for a *lodger alone*, or *two or more lodgers boarding together*.

Similar wording was used in 1871 and 1881.

These instructions were plainly designed to define the household as those persons in exclusive occupation of a room or rooms within a house. One would have expected, therefore, that a lodger given a household schedule of his or her own would have been treated as the head of a household in the relationship to head column but this was not in fact the case. In the examples supplied to the householders a boarder was shown as part of the household of the main occupier of a house. But in the enumerators' example whilst a solitary lodger was treated as a separate household (i.e. was marked off from the rest of the occupants of the house by a single oblique stroke), he was still described as a 'lodger' in the column for relationship to the head of the household. In one respect the solitary lodger was regarded as a separate household and in another as part of another co-residing group. This plainly caused confusion amongst householders and enumerators, and subsequently amongst historians.

In 1891 an attempt was made to eliminate this ambiguity. The definition of the occupier supplied to the enumerator dropped the term 'lodger' altogether.

> As a general rule, the term "occupier" is to be understood to apply *to the resident owner, or to a person who pays rent, whether for the whole of a house, or for a tenement consisting of one or more rooms.*

Similarly, the enumerator was instructed that a household schedule should be left with 'the occupier of a tenement living alone, or for two or more lodgers living together in one tenement'.

This appears to have been an attempt to raise the household status of lodgers not boarding with the families from whom they sublet. The effect was spoilt, however, by the example given to the enumerator. Here the lodger who formed a separate household in 1881, but was still a 'lodger' in relationship to the household head, had now become a 'head' in his own right. On the other hand, two other persons described as 'lodgers' in their relationship to the head of the family had appeared as part of another household. There was no indication as to how these differed from a 'boarder' in another household.

The situation was finally clarified in 1901 when the enumerators were instructed to leave a household schedule, amongst others;

a   for the head of the family occupying the whole or part of a house. NOTE – A *"family"* is held to include a man, and his wife and children (if any), also any relatives, visitors, servants, and *persons boarding with the family, and residing together under one roof.*

b   for a lodger (with or without family) separately occupying a room or rooms, *and not boarding with any family in the house.*

In the examples supplied to householders and enumerators, the term 'lodger' had disappeared. Every household was made up of a head, his relatives, and servants. One household contained a 'boarder'. The lodger boarding alone, or with other lodgers, had finally achieved full household status.

Definitions of the household used in census studies

The nineteenth-century census authorities plainly had a clear picture of what they thought a household ought to look like. It was made up of a husband and wife, their relations by birth or marriage, servants and apprentices. The family had exclusive possession of a house or apartment which they owned or rented from a landlord. Experience showed, of course, that this ideal was often not achieved in the working-class areas of towns and cities, where individuals and families sublet from other households. An attempt was made to make a distinction between the boarder who shared a common table with the household of which he was a member, and the lodger or group of lodgers who ate separately and constituted their own household. But the attachment to the Victorian ideal of the family was strong enough to ensure that the latter remained 'lodgers' in relationship to the head of the 'family' until at least 1891.

Anyone who has compared the work of differing enumerators is conscious that they interpreted these instructions differently. Some turned every lodger into a separate household, others always combined them with other households, whilst still others followed their own idiosyncratic conventions. The census authorities were themselves conscious of these problems. They believed that many lodgers who were treated as members of other households by the enumerators lived in quite separate social groups.[4]

Similar problems arise with regard to those persons described as 'visitors'. When did a distant relative or friend staying with a family cease to be on a visit and become a boarder or lodger? In cases where short stays in houses belonging to others were institutionalised, as in seaside resorts, a large proportion of the population might fall into this ambiguous category.

Faced with these problems historians have attempted to establish conventions for defining the household, or 'co-residing group', in the census. According to one set of conventions, in all nineteenth-century censuses from 1851 onwards the household should be defined as comprising all the names listed in an enumerator's book from one entry 'head' in the column headed 'relation to head of family' to the last name preceding the next entry 'head'. It is probably unwise to try and reconstruct households from the 1841 returns.

The only exceptions which have normally been made to this rule are first, occasional cases where other terms were used instead, and as a practical equivalent, of 'head'. In some of these cases the head was absent from home on census night but the enumerator recorded relationships by reference to him or her, with the result that the first entry for the household in the relationship to head column is 'wife', 'servant', 'wife, head absent', and so on. In other cases the head was at home but was identified by some term other than 'head'. Widows, for example, were occasionally recorded as 'widow'.

In such cases historians have applied the following rules. Where in 1851 a long or short line, and in other censuses a single or oblique stroke or a '1', is followed by an entry which suggests that the person first named is a head equivalent, or a head under another title, a new household has been counted. This exception has not been applied, however, in cases where this entry could reasonably refer to a relationship to the head of the previous household. In particular the term 'lodger' is never taken as a possible head equivalent, and historians have entered all lodgers as part of the previous household. The only exception to this is where 'lodger' follows the usual markers for a new house, and this is verified by the total number of houses at the bottom of the page, or by a new house address. A second exception to the general rule relating to households is where two successive individuals are both listed as 'head', or head equivalent, but no line or oblique stroke is drawn between them and there is no other indication of a new 'census family' (both, for example, have the same schedule number). Both are included in the same co-residing group, it being assumed that they share the headship.[5]

Given the evident confusion on the part of enumerators and householders, these general conventions are reasonable. It should be remembered, however, that they do not remove

4   *1891 preliminary census report*, p v.
5   Anderson, 'Standard tabulation procedures', pp 136–137.

the deficiencies in the data, they only allow one to treat these in the same manner. Many of the lodgers in the censuses from 1861 onwards, who under these conventions are treated as members of other households, were quite correctly shown by the enumerators as making up separate social entities. By indicating (with short lines or single strokes) that lodgers formed separate households whilst retaining the former designation in the relation to head column, enumerators were being consistent within the rules set down. The instructions given also changed over time and reinforced the separate household status of lodgers boarding on their own or with other lodgers. By defining the household in terms of the people grouped under the term 'head', the above conventions may tend to enlarge the average size of the household in the period 1861 to 1881 in comparison with other censuses. It is unfortunate, but perhaps understandable, that historians have established such conventions on the basis of the study of only two censuses (those of 1851 and 1861), and in apparent ignorance of some of the instructions given to the householders and enumerators.

Such problems are not overcome by using an alternative set of conventions in which one simply excludes boarders, lodgers, and visitors when analysing census data.[6] Since changing census instructions would tend to alter the characteristics of people who fell into such categories, one would not be excluding the same population at each census. A person or family who would be described as 'lodgers' in one census, might be raised to the status of separate households at the next. This procedure may certainly improve consistency within the returns of one census but would not necessarily do the same between differing censuses.

In most cases, and especially in rural areas, there are few difficulties as to what constitutes a census household. In cities, where there are problems with subletting and the proliferation of boarders and lodgers, the standard conventions noted above provide a rough and ready means of coping with the data. The larger the number of enumerators' books covered, the greater the likelihood that the distortions introduced by such conventions will be evened out, and comparisons between differing census populations facilitated. In comparing the work of individual enumerators, however, one must always be conscious of their individual idiosyncracies. In cases where there are a large number of lodgers or visitors in the population the results of any study which uses the above conventions should be treated with caution. This is especially true of comparisons across censuses for which the instructions regarding households differed.

Some of these problems may be overcome by noting the schedule numbers in the enumerators' returns. Each household schedule filled out was given a different number which from 1851 onwards run consecutively in the first column of the enumerators' books (see the examples in Appendix 3). These can be used to reconstruct how individual enumerators interpreted their instructions.

---

6   This appears to be the convention implicit in P Laslett and R Wall, *The household and family in past time* (London, 1974), pp 26–27, 34–36, 86–88; and in John Knodel, 'An exercise on household composition for use in courses in historical demography', *Local Population Studies*, XXIII (1979), pp 10–23.

10   Information relating to individuals

Although the falsification of census returns was a criminal offence, it is plain that the information collected was not always completely accurate. Certain types of information, such as name, are usually reliable but others, such as age, are only a very rough guide to nineteenth-century reality. This was not usually the result of deliberate evasion but reflected general ignorance of the precise information required, and prevailing levels of illiteracy. In an age when form filling and document keeping by the masses was unknown, many people did not know their precise date or place of birth, and hazarded a guess. Although modern researchers may be able to compare at one point in time the information supplied by householders at different censuses, such aides-memoire were not available to the Victorians themselves. In many cases the household schedules had to be filled out by the enumerators or neighbours, and these may have misunderstood accents, or made hasty and unwarranted assumptions. Illiterate householders and untrained enumerators may also have been confused as to the type of information required. In some cases unconventional marital relationships, or socially unacceptable physical and mental disabilities, may have been ignored or glossed over.

Although census data en masse gives a reliable approximation to the features of nineteenth-century society, one should not expect that all the information on individuals is strictly accurate or consistent over time. This is undoubtably more of a problem for the family historian than for other students of the period, and can sometimes be overcome by tracing individuals through more than one census. Those who deal in aggregate data can often take solace in the fact that any discrepancies are usually within reasonable bounds, and may cancel each other out.

The information relating to occupations is perhaps the most difficult to interpret, and the data in this column is considered separately in Chapter 11.

Names

Names are perhaps the least problematic element of the information relating to individuals in the census. In 1841 only the first christian name was to be given but in 1851 the enumerator was instructed that the initial of the second christian name 'may be inserted'. From 1891 onwards the instruction was that this initial 'must be inserted'. If a name was not known, 'n.k.' was to be substituted. For several persons in succession with the same surname, 'do' for 'ditto' was to be used for every surname but the first.[1]

---

1   See the examples of the enumerators' books which can be found in the relevant census classes for 1841 to 1881. Examples of those for 1891 can be found in RG 27/6, Items 71, 73, 74. The RG 27 volume for 1901 is 'Wanting' but the Office of Population Censuses and Surveys has supplied the author with a copy of the first five pages of an enumeration book. These contain printed pro forma material relating to fictitious persons rather than any information on named individuals.

Differences between names do appear from census to census but are usually not very frequent. They may reflect copying errors made by the enumerator, inverting christian and surname, using one too many 'dittos', leaving out letters, and so on. Equally they may reflect the differing ways in which enumerators heard and interpreted names when interrogating illiterate householders on their doorstep. In this way 'Ann Apling' becomes 'Ann Aplin', 'Ellinor Daniels' becomes 'Ellen Daniel', 'Richard Meirieth' becomes 'Richard Meredith', and so on. One can usually establish that these are one and the same person by the coincidence of other personal details and those of the other members of the household.

Cases can occasionally be found where there are inexplicable differences between the head's surname and that of his or her family: William Simpson has Sarah Lee as his wife, although his children are called Simpson; Henry Steel has Hannah Hall as his wife but his son is called William Hall.[2] A variety of explanations can be put forward for such anomalies but these may have more to do with problems in the relationship to head column than with the names of the individuals concerned.

Relationship to head of family

The information in the relationship to head column is sometimes more difficult to interpret. This reflects nineteenth-century usages which were different from those of today, and confusion as to the exact status of individuals in the household. Fortunately, such problems are usually restricted to a discrete number of terms, and can often be spotted with a little care.

In 1841 there was no relationship column in the census schedules. Enumerators were merely told to 'Set down one after the other those who have the same surname, beginning with the heads of the family, and put no others between them'.[3]

Certain conventions have been established by social historians in order to assign relationships to the members of 1841 households.[4] These are very rough and ready rules and great caution should be taken when using them to compare differing populations in the 1841 census, or to compare these results with later censuses. It may be even more difficult to use these assumptions for genealogical purposes. It is assumed that the first listed person is the head. To allocate persons of the same surname, the following rules are applied:

    a the first listed woman within fifteen years of the head's age is assumed to be his wife. Other women, provided that (from consideration of their ages) they are born when the head and wife (where applicable) were aged not below fifteen and not over fifty, are assumed to be daughters. Any other women are treated as relatives;

    b other males bearing the same name are regarded as sons, provided that they too were born when the head and wife were aged not less than fifteen and not more than fifty. Other males are regarded as relatives.

2   P M Tillott, 'Sources of inaccuracy in the 1851 and 1861 censuses', in *Nineteenth-century society*, ed. Wrigley, p 106.

3   1841 and 1851 Census Returns (PRO: HO 107).

4   W A Armstrong, 'Social structure from the early census returns', in *An introduction to English historical demography*, ed. E A Wrigley (London, 1966), pp 229–230.

These conventions become more difficult to apply, of course, where the first person in a household is a woman.

Further rules cover the allocation of those not bearing the head's surname. Domestic servants are taken as being all those so described in the occupation column, unless they have the same name as the head (in which case they are taken to be children or relatives), or unless the head of the household is also by occupation described as a servant (whereupon they are regarded as lodgers). All those not covered by the above rules are placed in a residual category of lodgers.

In 1851 a relationship column was added to the household schedule. This carried the instruction, 'State whether wife, son, daughter or other relative, visitor or servant'. In 1861 'boarder, etc.' was added to the list, as was 'Head' in 1871. The instruction remained the same for the rest of the century, except for the suppression of the 'etc.' after boarder in 1881. At various times certain abbreviations were suggested, 'daur.' for daughter, 'serv.' for servant, 'F.-in-Law' and 'M.-in-Law' for father-in-law and mother-in-law respectively, and so on.[5]

The first thing to note is that the headship of a household was a social position and did not necessarily reflect priority in terms of biological descent. Thus, in one household an aged widow might be described as head but in another case a son or daughter who had taken over running the affairs of the group might be so designated. Occasionally two men or women sharing a set of rooms might both be put down as joint heads. Sometimes the usual head of the household was absent and this was denoted by the first person in the household being described as a wife, son, servant, or some other term.

Nineteenth-century usages for kin relationships were sometimes different from those of today. Relationships by marriage appear to cause particular problems. A brother-in-law or son-in-law could be described as 'brother' or 'son', whilst a 'daughter-in-law' might mean a step-daughter. Similarly, the offspring of married children resident in the household were sometimes called 'son' or 'daughter' rather than grandchild; the relationship referring to their parents rather than the head-grandparent. The term 'nurse child' is also ambiguous since it could cover a child sleeping in a house for one night, or a case of adoption.

The confusion between lodger and boarder, and the ambiguities relating to visitors, have already been noted (Chapter 9). Such designations probably have to be accepted at face value but relationship data from enumeration districts with large numbers of boarders, lodgers and visitors should be treated with caution.

The term 'servant' can cause confusion, especially since it could also appear in the occupational column. Service in the nineteenth century was a legal relationship between master and servant rather than a defined set of tasks. Apprentices, shop workers, domestic servants, and living-in agricultural labourers could be regarded as servants. Since it was

---

5   See the examples of the enumerators' books which can be found in the relevant census classes for 1841 to 1881. Examples of those for 1891 can be found in RG 27/6, Items 71, 73, 74. The RG 27 volume for 1901 is 'Wanting' but the Office of Population Censuses and Surveys has supplied the author with a copy of the first five pages of an enumeration book. These contain printed pro forma material relating to fictitious persons rather than any information on named individuals.

the nature of the social relationship which was important, the distinction between a paid employee and the poor country cousin who did housework in return for her keep must have been a fine one. Similarly, the extent to which the relationship 'servant' and the occupational designation 'housekeeper' was used to conceal unconventional, or complicated, marital relationships is difficult to quantify. People with domestic service occupations were also not necessarily servants in the households in which they lived; they could be lodgers and kin who were unemployed, or who went out to work in other houses during the day. The interpretation of occupational data on domestic servants is examined in more detail in the next chapter.

On occasion the meaning of the term 'relationship' could be hopelessly misconstrued, as in the case of the farm labourer living in a shed at the bottom of a farmer's garden who described his relationship to the head of the family as 'friendly'.[6]

Marital status

The 1841 census did not ask for information on marital status but this became a standard feature from 1851 onwards.[7] In that year the householder was instructed to, 'Write "Married", "Widower", or "Unmarried", against the names of all Persons except Young Children' in the column headed 'Condition'. The examples supplied to the enumerators showed the use of the abbreviations, 'Mar.', 'Widr.' and 'U.' for such marital conditions.

In 1861 'Un.' was indicated as the abbreviation for unmarried, whilst 'W' for widow was also introduced. In 1871 'Unm.' was substituted for 'Un.'. At the following census the abbreviations were as before, although the column heading now became, 'Condition as to marriage'. In 1891 the term 'Single', abbreviated to 'S', was substituted for that of 'Unmarried'. The abbreviation for 'Widow' now became 'Wid.'.

The information supplied in this column is usually self-explanatory but there may be some cases of doubtful enumeration. According to the *1881 census report* the number of wives in the population exceeded the number of husbands by 61,064.[8] Some of these women may have had husbands who were out of the country but the exact marital status of others may be in some doubt.

The number of 'married' women under the age of twenty years whose husbands were absent is especially high. This might reflect the absence of spouses in the armed forces or merchant marine, or those cases where young women were living at home until they and their husbands could afford to set up a home. On the other hand, were such women only engaged? In the quite common case of mature married women who were also described as heads of households, is one to assume that their husbands were away from home, that they would have been described as heads even if their husbands had been at home, or that

6   RG 9/1783, f 35, p 22.
7   See the examples of the enumerators' books which can be found in the relevant census classes for 1841 to 1881. Examples of those for 1891 can be found in RG 27/6, Items 71, 73, 74. The RG 27 volume for 1901 is 'Wanting' but the Office of Population Censuses and Surveys has supplied the author with a copy of the first five pages of an enumeration book. These contain printed pro forma material relating to fictitious persons rather than any information on named individuals.
8   *1881 census report*, PP 1883 LXXX [c. 3797], p 23.

they were separated? Did some women still regard themselves as married to husbands who were dead? On the other hand, might some separated husbands and wives enumerate themselves as 'Widow' or 'Widower' in order to hide feelings of shame? These and similar questions must remain in the realms of speculation, and each case must be considered on its merits.

Age recording

The recording of ages is without doubt one of the most problematic features of the manuscript census returns. The ages reported in the census must be regarded as only rough approximations to the actual facts. In a period before systematic record keeping many people had only a rough idea of their date of birth, and in some cases there may have been temptations to give incorrect information. In very general terms one can say that the majority of ages stated will be consistent from census to census. A person aged forty in the census of 1851 will appear as fifty in 1861. In a sizeable minority of cases, however, there will not be ten years between the two ages recorded. Most discrepancies will be in the order of one or two years but larger differences are by no means uncommon. The censuses were taken on differing dates each year (see Appendix 1) but the differences were too small to have caused the age discrepancies observed. In some cases, of course, such discrepancies will be 'self righting'; those who describe themselves as thirty at one census and thirty-six at the next, might describe themselves as fifty ten years later.

In the case of Preston, Anderson has calculated that whilst fifty-three per cent of a sample of people reported consistently between the censuses of 1851 and 1861, only four per cent of the ages were 'wrong' by more than two years.[9] Similarly, Tillott found that in the parishes of Hathersage (Derbyshire) and Braithwell (Yorkshire), consistency rates of sixty-one per cent and sixty-eight per cent respectively were recorded between censuses. On the other hand, five per cent in each parish were inconsistent by more than two years.[10]

In the case of Colyton in Devon in the four censuses between 1851 and 1881 all households headed by someone with a surname beginning with A and D were traced by the author.[11] Out of fifty-five observations of the ages of men between censuses, none was more than two years discrepant. In the case of the fifty-seven observations for women, four per cent were more than two years out. Members of the Cambridge Group for the History of Population and Social Structure have studied the age recording of all the inhabitants of Colyton between 1851 and 1861. In the case of males, they discovered that only 51.5% recorded themselves as ten years older in 1861, but only 6.9% were discrepant by more than two years. In the case of women the equivalent figures were 52.4% and 9.5%.[12]

A similar analysis was undertaken for the parish of Llangefni in Anglesey, where all households headed by someone with a surname beginning with A, D or M were traced

---

9   M Anderson, 'The study of family structure', in *Nineteenth-century society*, ed. Wrigley, p 75.
10   Tillott, 'Sources of inaccuracy', p 108.
11   1851, HO 107/1862; 1861 Census Returns (PRO: RG 9): RG 9/1373; 1871 Census Returns (PRO: RG 10): RG 10/2035–2036; 1881 Census Returns (PRO: RG 11): RG 11/2129.
12   The author would like to thank Jean Robin of the Cambridge Group for supplying him with the results of her research in this area.

over the period 1851 to 1881.[13] Of the thirty-nine observations of the ages of men between two censuses, ten per cent were discrepant by more than two years. In the case of women, out of forty-four observations only fifty-five per cent showed a gap of exactly ten years, and twelve per cent showed discrepancies of more than two years. The standard of age reporting plainly varied from place to place.

The instructions regarding age reporting given in 1841 were rather confusing. The householder was told to

> Write in figures the age of every person, opposite to their names, in one of the columns headed "Age of Males" or "Age of Females" according to their sex. For persons aged 15 years and upwards it is sufficient to state within what period of five years their age is, writing down the *lowest* number of that period: thus, for persons aged 15 and under 20, write 15— for 20 and under 25, write 20— for 25 and under 30 write 25— for 30 and under 35 write 30—, and so on up to the greatest age; but the *exact age* may be stated if the person prefers it. For persons under 15, write the number of years; for infants under one year the number of months.[14]

The enumerators were instructed to treat the ages reported in a slightly different manner. The age of every person under fifteen was to be given exactly as stated. Those aged fifteen or above were to have their ages expressed to the lowest term of five years within which their age fell. Those aged twenty to twenty-four years, for example, were to be recorded as twenty. If no more could be ascertained respecting the age of a person than that they were a child or a grown up, the enumerator was to write 'under 20' or 'above 20' according to the circumstances. The ages given were, therefore, only very approximate, and there must have been ample room for confusion.

In 1851 householders were given no general instructions regarding age reporting, although the appropriate column in the household schedule was headed 'Age [last birthday]'. The householder was instructed, however, that for infants under one year 'state the Age in *Months*, writing "*Under 1 Month*", "*1 Month*", "*2 Months*", etc.'. The enumerator was instructed to enter 'the number of *years* simply' in the ages column, except in those cases where the age was expressed in months, when 'Mo.' had to be written after the figures. The instructions in subsequent censuses followed this general form.[15] From 1851, therefore, the instructions to the householders and enumerators were fairly clear and straightforward, although one cannot be certain to what extent individuals read these instructions carefully, or could read them at all.

The inconsistencies in the data partly reflected the ignorance of many people respecting their exact age, leading them to make a guess. When doing so there appears to have been a tendency for people to round their ages to multiples of ten and five, to 30, 40, 50, 60 etc., and to a lesser extent to 35, 45, 55, etc. This was at the expense of contiguous years, although there is evidence that there was a greater tendency to round ages down than upwards. It has been suggested that this tendency set in after the age of twenty years.[16] It

13   1851, HO 107/2520; 1861, RG 9/4362; 1871, RG 10/5742; 1881, RG 11/5586.
14   RG 27/1, p 58.
15   HO 45/3579.
16   *1881 census report*, p 17.

has also been reported in one study that there appears to be a rather high coincidence between the ages of husband and wife, which may indicate that married couples guessed at an age together.[17]

It is important, therefore, to select age bands or cohorts with care when aggregating age data. Genealogists also need to treat the ages given in the census as approximations, and should look at a range of years for the registration of births in ecclesiastical records. If a man or woman is said to be fifty in the 1851 census, it is reasonably likely that they were born in the period 1799 to 1803.

Similarly, there appears to be a general tendency to think in terms of age next birthday rather than age last birthday, especially in the case of children. A child of seven years five months became eight, because they were 'in their eighth year'. This is especially serious in the case of children aged under one year, and the numbers recorded as in their first year of life are therefore underestimated. This may be partly explained by the fact that this was how ages often had to be stated for insurance purposes. Alternatively there may have been some desire not to 'waste' some months of the age. This tendency may well have been present up to the age of fifteen years. The under-enumeration of children under one may also reflect an erroneous impression on the part of some parents that new-born children who had not been christened or named did not need to be included in the census.[18]

There may have been pressures to falsify some ages. It has been suggested that there was a tendency to raise the age of children in their early teens since under the Factory Acts children were not allowed to work until they were thirteen years old. It is also suggested that a number of girls aged ten to thirteen exaggerated their ages in order to get into domestic service but that this tendency rapidly declined after the age of nineteen.[19]

On the other hand, the *1851 census report* suggested that some women depressed their ages after the early twenties because that was the age at which women in England usually got married, 'either because they are quite unconscious of the silent lapse of time, – or because their imaginations linger over the hours of that age, – or because they choose, foolishly, to represent themselves as younger than they really were, at the scandalous risk of bringing the statements of the whole of their country women into discredit'. There may, however, have been a countervailing tendency for young domestic servants to exaggerate their ages in order to gain higher wages.[20]

There is evidence that some of the very elderly exaggerated their ages. But this probably applied markedly only in the age groups above eighty-five years. There may have been a tendency for working-class men in their fifties to describe themselves as over sixty. Those over that age, if still able-bodied, were entitled to outdoor relief on the poor law. If they were inmates of workhouses they also had certain privileges, such as a better diet.

---

17   W T R Pryce, 'The census as a major source for the study of Flintshire society in the nineteenth century', *The Journal of the Flintshire Historical Society*, XXVI (1973–74), p 127.

18   *1881 census report*, p 18; *1891 census report*, p 28; *1901 census report*, p 51; W A Armstrong, 'The census enumerators' books: a commentary', in *The census and social structure*, ed. Lawton, p 35.

19   *1881 census report*, p 17; *1891 census report*, p 28; *1901 census report*, p 67.

20   *1851 census report: population tables, II*, PP 1852–53 LXXXVIII, Pt 1 [1691–I.], pp xxiv–xxv; *1901 census report*, p 51.

These observations raise the question of how far people believed that the census was confidential. Since enumerators were often local government officers or teachers, it would not be unusual if some working-class households were cautious about giving what might be regarded as awkward information.[21]

There appears to be a tendency for the wealthier classes to record their ages more consistently but little work has been done on the subject. Class influences were plainly complex. Whilst working-class men in their late fifties may have exaggerated their age, members of the middle classes may have reduced their own to ward off the threat of retirement.[22]

It has also been suggested that small, rural parishes may have better age recording than urban areas with a more mobile population. In such rural areas the closeness of the community may have made the mis-statement of ages more difficult, although this is hardly borne out in the case of Llangefni mentioned above.[23]

The *Census reports* after 1881 comment on the decreasing tendency of young girls to exaggerate their ages. The age reporting amongst the very young and the elderly is also said to have improved. But this was apparently not the case with the tendency for women to record themselves as in their early twenties. This improvement may reflect the spread of compulsory education in the period after the 1870 Education Act.[24]

Many of these patterns noted in age data are of an aggregative nature. They are what can be observed in the published age tables after balancing out many opposing tendencies. There is no guarantee that these patterns will be manifested in every population, and certainly not in the case of every individual.

Sex

The recording of the sex of individuals was intimately bound up with age recording. This may reflect the desire of the officers of the GRO to use the data for the construction of separate life tables for men and women. The practice creates some minor problems for the interpretation of the data supplied.

In 1841 there was no separate column for sex on the householders' returns. Instead there were two columns for age; one for males and one for females. This layout was repeated in the enumerators' returns. From 1851 onwards the householders' schedules contained a column for sex in which 'F' for female and 'M' for male were to be inserted. There was then a separate age column. The enumerators' books, however, retained the double age column.

21   *1881 census report*, p 18; *1891 census report*, p 28. On the general problems of obtaining information from working-class households in cities, see the testimony of Charles James White, a census enumerator in Mile End in 1881, before the 1890 Treasury Committee on the Census; *1890 report of the Treasury Committee on the Census*, QQ 1850–1859.

22   D Thomson, 'Age reporting by the elderly and the nineteenth century census', *Local Population Studies*, XXV (1980), p 21.

23   Thomson, 'Age reporting by the elderly', p 23.

24   *1901 census report*, pp 51–58.

The enumerators had to combine two pieces of information, on sex and age, from the household schedules when filling in their returns.[25]

Occasionally the enumerators made a slip and inserted the age in the wrong column. These problems can usually be detected by the subsequent amendments made by the census clerks, or by checking the name column. The *1891 census report* noted, however, that these slips were not random. Each enumerator had a tendency to make errors in the same column. The majority of those making errors tended to put the ages of males in the column for women.[26] The number of cases involved, however, was very small.

Birthplace data

The information relating to birthplaces in the census is of considerable importance to all students of nineteenth-century society but is essential for the historian of population migration and for the genealogist. The latter needs this information in order to be able to follow his or her ancestors back through the ecclesiastical records of baptisms, marriages and burials. Despite its importance very little work has been done on the accuracy of this information, especially since there are few other sources to check it against. This is disturbing since what research has been done indicates that the census is not always a reliable source.

The quality of the birthplace data in the 1841 census is far from satisfactory. The household schedule contained two columns for this information headed 'Whether born in the same county', and 'Whether born in Scotland, Ireland, or Foreign Parts'. Householders were instructed to write 'yes' or 'no' in the first column. In the second column they were to write 'Scotland', 'Ireland' or 'Foreigner'. The latter designation only referred to those born outside the UK who were not British subjects. Those born abroad who were British subjects were to be entered in the first column with the word 'no'. The number of British subjects born outside the UK but resident there in 1841 cannot, therefore, be calculated. The enumerators were instructed to abbreviate these entries when copying them into their books, using 'Y', 'N', 'S', 'I', and 'F' respectively.[27]

In 1851 more informative answers were required. In the case of those born in England, householders were to indicate first the county, and then the town or parish of birth. This order was to be followed in all subsequent Victorian censuses. In the case of those born in

25 Examples of the household schedules can be found in various PRO record classes: 1841, RG 27/1, pp 56–57; 1851, HO 45/3579; 1861, RG 27/3, Item 2; 1871, RG 27/4, Item 5; 1881, RG 27/5, Item 5; 1891, RG 27/6, Item 68; 1901, RG 19/11. Examples of the enumerators' books can be found in the relevant census classes for 1841 to 1881. Examples of those of 1891 can be found in RG 27/6, Items 71, 73, 74. The RG 27 volume for 1901 is 'Wanting' but the Office of Population Censuses and Surveys has supplied the author with a copy of the first five pages of an enumeration book. These contain printed pro forma material relating to fictitious persons rather than any information on named individuals.
26 *1891 census report*, p 25.
27 Examples of the household schedules can be found in various PRO record classes: 1841, RG 27/1, pp 56–57; 1851, HO 45/3579; 1861, RG 27/3, Item 2; 1871, RG 27/4, Item 5; 1881, RG 27/5, Item 5; 1891, RG 27/6, Item 68; 1901, RG 19/11. Examples of the enumerators' books can be found in the relevant census classes for 1841 to 1881. Examples of those for 1891 can be found in RG 27/6, Items 71, 73, 74. The RG 27 volume for 1901 is 'Wanting' but the Office of Population Censuses and Surveys has supplied the author with a copy of the first five pages of an enumeration book. These contain printed pro forma material relating to fictitious persons rather than any information on named individuals.

Scotland, Ireland, the British colonies, the East Indies or foreign parts, the country of birth was to be stated. The term 'British Subjects' was to be added to the latter where appropriate. Interestingly, Wales was not mentioned in the instructions on this matter until 1891, when the principality was treated in the same manner as England.

Some other minor changes were introduced in the course of the century. In 1861 a distinction was to be made between 'British Subject' and 'Naturalised British Subject'. In 1871 those born in Scotland, Ireland, the British colonies, or the East Indies, were to state the country or colony of birth; and those born in foreign parts the particular state or country. The 1901 census broke the population down into four groups in the following manner:

State the Birthplace of each person

1   If in England and Wales, the County and Town, or Parish.
2   If in Scotland or Ireland, the name of the County.
3   If in a British Colony or Dependency, the name of the Colony or Dependency.
4   If in a Foreign Country, the name of the Country, and whether the person be a "British Subject", a "Naturalised British Subject", or a "Foreign Subject" specifying nationality such as "French", "German", etc.

One may have doubts as to the extent to which householders understood the instructions with regard to those born outside the UK but those relating to people born in England, Scotland and Ireland appear fairly straightforward. It may be something of a surprise, therefore, to discover the chief clerk of the GRO claiming in 1910 that

the birthplace tables were probably the most inaccurate of any of the census tables but feared they could be dispensed with as some people seemed to attach considerable importance to the figures. Not only did a great many people not know in which county they were born but a place which was not a town might easily have been a small village at the time of the birth of persons aged 20 years and upwards who were enumerated in other towns.[28]

The chief clerk may have been exaggerating the deficiencies of the returns but they must certainly not be regarded as completely accurate. In the case of mid-nineteenth century Preston, Anderson has shown that of the 475 persons he traced in two successive censuses fourteen per cent had a discrepancy in birthplace between the two years. Some of these were not of great importance but in half of these cases migrants into Preston became non-migrants and vice versa.[29] If one looks at the samples from Colyton and Llangefni mentioned in a previous section, similar problems arise. In the former case out of 112 observations across censuses there were ten discrepancies. In the case of Llangefni there were twenty-three discrepancies out of eighty-three observations. Similar work on the birthplace of household heads in Colyton in 1851 undertaken by the Cambridge Group

28   RG 19/48B, p 69.
29   Anderson, 'The study of family structure', p 75.

reveals that 15.7% of male heads changed their place of birth, at one or more censuses, between 1851 and 1881.[30] The equivalent figure for female heads was six per cent. A study by Razzell indicated that levels of discrepancies may have been higher in urban than in rural areas. In Bethnal Green between 1851 and 1861, seventy-five double entries out of 440 traced showed such discrepancies, a rate of seventeen per cent.[31]

As Anderson points out, many of these discrepancies are minor and easily explained. Variations in the spelling of place names were common, especially in Wales and Cornwall. Enumerators unfamiliar with the local accent, or with the pronunciation of a place name, might note the latter phonetically, as they heard it on the doorstep. Some birthplaces, for example, lack the first letters because of a dropped 'h'. Long Welsh placenames can cause particular problems if they were truncated. A birthplace given as 'Llanfair' might refer to Llanfair Dyffryn Clwyd or Llanfair Talhaiarn; 'Llanrhaiadr' could be intended for Llanrhaiadr-yn-Kinmerch or Llanrhaiadr-yn-Mochnant. One must also be careful not to read 'N.K.' (not known) for 'U.K.'. Sometimes the change reflects a greater or lesser degree of specificity; 'Colyton' in one census becomes the tithing of 'Colyford' within the parish of Colyton in the next.[32] But in a significant minority of cases the parish of birth changes. In Colyton and Llangefni these changes mostly reflected the substitution of the name of neighbouring parishes for the original place of birth, and were invariably within the same county. Genealogists would be advised, therefore, to check the birthplace of ancestors in more than one census before going to the local parish records.

Occasionally the grasp of British geography shown by householders and enumerators was not strong. Entries such as 'Lancashire, Kendal', and 'Lancashire, Penrith', and the placing of Birmingham freely in a number of Midland counties, testify to these problems. As has been noted before, however, the nineteenth century was a period of great change in local government, and some changes in the county of birth may indicate boundary changes.

It should also be noted that there was a tendency to record the place of residence, or the earliest one which could be remembered, as the place of birth. In institutions such as workhouses there appears to be a propensity on the part of some returning officers to give the location of the institution as the place of birth. In the case of extremely ill people in hospitals, or of the senile elderly in workhouses, such practices are perhaps understandable.

On the other hand, Wrigley has calculated that in 1851 between 135 and 150 individuals in Colyton were inaccurately claiming Colyton birth, at a time when the total of those stated as being born outside the parish was only 1,032. He also notes the tendency of recent migrants to change their place of birth to Colyton.[33] This pattern may have something to do with the workings of the poor law. In order to obtain poor relief in one's place of

---

30   Information supplied by Jean Robin of the Cambridge Group for the History of Population and Social Structure.

31   P E Razzell, 'The evaluation of baptism as a form of birth registration through cross-matching census and parish register data: a study in methodology', *Population Studies*, XXVI (1972), p 123.

32   In the case of the Cambridge Group's calculations the substitution of Colyton and Colyford has not been counted as a change of birthplace.

33   E A Wrigley, 'Baptism coverage in early nineteenth-century England: the Colyton area', *Population Studies*, XXIX (1975), pp 299–306.

residence it was necessary to prove 'settlement' in the parish. One did so through either claiming birth there, or through living there for a set period. Although the latter gave the poor the right not to be 'removed' to their place of birth, claiming one's place of residence as one's birthplace may have been seen as an extra insurance against this.[34] This tends to reduce the overall level of migration shown in the census, and should be borne in mind by historians when discussing population movements in this period.

It must also be remembered that the census only indicates the place of birth and the place of residence on census night. It does not indicate all movements between these dates. A person recorded as having been born in their place of residence may have travelled round the world between the date of their birth and census night. Such movements can sometimes be detected by the birthplaces of children. It is essential to understand that the census data merely provides a picture of the final results of migration and not a full record of the migration itself.

The exact status of those born abroad is sometimes difficult to determine. It was generally believed in the GRO that people did not understand the instructions relating to naturalisation.[35] The number of foreigners by both birth and nationality may be inflated by the omission of 'British Subject' or 'Naturalised British Subject'. On the other hand, it was suggested that some foreigners, especially refugees, may have falsified their returns by claiming British birth or nationality in order to avoid further persecution. Certainly the GRO was continually pestered by foreign embassies to supply the names and addresses of their nationals resident in the country. But the GRO refused such requests, and generally thought that this problem was not very serious.[36]

Medical disabilities

Despite the importance which the GRO placed upon the collection of information relating to medical disabilities, there is every indication that the results obtained were untrustworthy. The reasons for this inaccuracy are interesting in themselves but also provide examples, writ large, of problems found elsewhere in the census data.

The first questions about medical disabilities were introduced in the 1851 census. Householders were asked to state if members of their household were deaf and dumb, or blind. The same question was asked in 1861 but 'from birth' had to be added if the affliction was congenital. In 1871 householders were also to indicate if members of the household were imbeciles, idiots or lunatics. The term 'from birth' was also to be added in appropriate cases. The examples of how to fill out the form muddied the waters, however, by containing 'Blind from Small-pox' as an entry in the appropriate column. The 1881 instructions were the same as in 1871 but 'Blind from Small-pox' was removed from the example. The instructions for 1891 and 1901 were similar to those for 1881, although 'from childhood' was substituted for 'from birth', and in 1901 'feeble minded' for 'idiot'.

34   T MacKay, *A history of the English poor law* (London, 1904), III, pp 341–366; K D M Snell, *Annals of the labouring poor. Social change and agrarian England 1600-1900* (Cambridge, 1985), pp 71–84.

35   *1891 census report*, p 64.

36   General Register Office: Letter Books (PRO: RG 29): RG 29/9, pp 72, 104; *1891 census report*, p 66.

Householders were also warned not to use vague terms such as 'afflicted' or 'infirm'.[37]

Although the census authorities were fairly sanguine about the results in 1851, they appear to have become increasingly aware of their deficiencies as the century drew to a close. By the 1880s they no longer defended the statistics produced as accurate but simply argued that since the level of inaccuracy was probably constant across the country, the returns could be used for comparative purposes.[38]

The main problem was that parents, or other family members, were unwilling to admit that their children or relatives had medical disabilities. In the case of very young children, parents may have been unaware of any medical problems. Even as they grew older it may have been difficult for parents to admit to themselves, let alone to the census authorities, that their children were mentally or physically disabled. After the age of fifteen such problems may have declined. In 1881 the census authorities obtained from the managers of a large asylum the addresses of the families of those persons admitted as 'idiots' in the year commencing with the day of the census. They discovered that in half the cases of those aged five years to fourteen years, no mention was made in the census schedules as to the existence of any mental incapacity.[39] When 'feeble minded' was substituted for 'idiot' in 1901, the number of persons recorded as having a mental disability rose markedly. This was put down to the fact that the former term was much less derogatory than the latter.[40] The substitution of terms makes it extremely difficult to make any comparisons between 1901 and previous censuses.

The other general problem with the returns was confusion over the exact nature of the data required. Householders, many illiterate, were being asked to give information about medical disabilities without any precise definitions of the terms employed. In the case of blindness, no indication was given as to whether a person had to be totally blind to be included, or whether a partial lack of sight could be enumerated. For practical purposes most people probably regarded someone as blind if they were unable to direct their path by means of sight. Popularly the term 'born blind' appears to have included those who had gone blind at a very early age as well as those blind at birth. Similarly, the census asked for information on those who were deaf and dumb, but people put down relatives who were deaf, and those who could not speak whilst retaining the faculty of hearing.[41]

The exact definitions of terms such as 'lunatic', 'imbecile', 'idiot' and 'feeble minded', are extremely problematic. According to the *1881 census report*,

> No accurate line of demarcation can be drawn between the several conditions indicated by these terms. Speaking generally, however, the term idiot is applied in popular usage simply to those who suffer from congenital mental deficiency, and the term imbecile to persons who have fallen in later life into a state of chronic dementia.

---

37   Examples of the household schedules can be found in various PRO record classes: 1841, RG 27/1, pp 56–57; 1851, HO 45/3579; 1861, RG 27/3, Item 2; 1871, RG 27/4, Item 5; 1881, RG 27/5, Item 5; 1891, RG 27/6, Item 68; 1901, RG 19/11.

38   *1881 census report*, p 69.

39   *1881 census report*, pp 68-69.

40   *1901 census report*, pp 155-156.

41   *1861 census report*, pp 47, 55; *1891 census report*, p 70; *1901 census report*, p 153.

But it is certain that neither this nor any other definite distinction between the terms was rigorously observed in the schedules, and consequently no attempt has been made by us to separate imbeciles from idiots. The term lunatic also is used with some vagueness, and probably some persons suffering from congenital idiocy, and many more suffering from dementia, were returned under this name.[42]

One cannot be certain, therefore, to what extent the usage of these terms corresponded to the later distinctions made between mental illness and mental disability. Or did people adhere to the seventeenth-century definition of a lunatic as a person who had lucid periods, while an idiot did not? Within the field of mental disabilities, early twentieth-century medical usage came to use the term idiot for someone who was incapable of attending to his own personal needs. An imbecile could perform some simple functions of self help, whilst having only a limited grasp of ideas. How far these definitions would have been popularly used in the nineteenth century is extremely difficult to determine. The use of the term 'feeble minded' in 1901 appears to have led to a greater willingness to record senile dementia amongst the elderly.

The lack of care in filling in this column is made plain by the inclusion of information regarding afflictions other than those required. In one area of Wales, for example, the following entries amongst others were recorded; 'invalid for eight years', 'rheumatic cripple', 'unhealthy from birth', 'not well', 'helpless', 'infirmity', 'pleurisy', 'illness entire', 'tubercular', 'cripple from birth-one leg'.[43] But there is no guarantee that such states were recorded consistently. Confusion may also be caused by the use made by the census clerks of this column for ticking off birthplaces as they went through the books.

The indications are, therefore, that the information relating to medical disabilities is very untrustworthy. Aggregate analyses based on this data may have some uses for comparative purposes but the results cannot be used to estimate the overall extent, or relative importance, of the various medical disabilities suffered by Victorians.

Language spoken in Wales and Monmouthshire

In Chapter 5 the special arrangements for enumerating the Welsh-speaking population in Wales and Monmouthshire have been briefly described. Household schedules in Welsh were produced from 1841 onwards. Until 1891 the enumeration books used and the questions asked in the principality were the same as those in England. In that year a new question on the language spoken was introduced but was confined solely to Wales and Monmouthshire. The household schedules (both in English and Welsh) and enumeration books used there in 1891 and 1901 have an extra column for this information as compared to those used in England. The number of Welsh speakers who were living in England cannot, therefore, be calculated.

42   *1881 census report*, p 66.
43   A A Benjamin, 'Human afflictions: a study of the north Ceredigion census returns, 1851–1871', *Ceredigion*, X (1985), pp 155–156.

In the column in their schedules headed 'Language Spoken' householders were to put 'English' if they only spoke English, 'Welsh' if they only spoke Welsh, and 'Both' if they spoke Welsh and English. In 1901, however, returns were not to be made for children under three years of age.

The results obtained by means of these questions do not appear to have been very trustworthy. Since there was no standard laid down as to the degree of proficiency required in speaking English, people in certain districts believed that if they spoke Welsh preferentially or habitually, and only spoke English occasionally or poorly, they were justified in returning themselves as speaking Welsh only. It was noted that children in schools which taught English were put down as being able to speak Welsh only, as were infants of only a few months, or even days, old. The GRO hinted that this may have been due to the effects of Welsh nationalism but the usual confusion on the part of householders as to the exact information required was probably a more potent source of error.[44]

The 1901 exclusion of children aged under three years may have improved the returns to some extent but they must still be handled with some caution. They can be used to obtain the total number of persons who could speak Welsh, with or without English, by combining those who were returned as speaking Welsh only with those who were bilingual. One is less justified in using them to calculate the number who could not speak English in some form or other.

In both censuses some people indicated that they spoke languages other than Welsh or English. The appropriate column in the household schedule was headed 'Language Spoken', and although it was plainly intended to relate to Welsh-speaking this could be interpreted in a broader sense. But householders were only specifically asked to indicate Welsh or English speaking, and many of those speaking other languages will probably have made nil returns.

---

44   *1891 census report*, pp 81–82; *Explanatory letter of the registrar general of England and Wales relative to the census of 1891*, PP 1894 LXIX [331].

11 Occupations in the censuses

Introduction

The occupational information recorded in the nineteenth-century censuses is of fundamental importance for reconstructing Victorian society. In an age before censuses of production, or detailed sociological investigations, this is the most comprehensive source for the detailed statistical investigation of economic and social structure. There are a considerable number of problems, however, with the occupational returns which need to be considered before the source is utilised in this manner. This is not to disparage its use but merely to urge caution when dealing with certain economic or social groups.

It should be noted that, at least until 1891, householders were not asked to indicate the paid economic activities of the members of their household, they were asked to give their 'Rank, Profession, or Occupation'. This could be taken to imply personal social status, rather than a description of economic activity. The only innovation in 1891 was to drop 'Rank' from the heading. It was only in the twentieth century that the census asked for a separate description of the nature of the business of one's employer as well as one's own personal occupation.[1]

It is also essential to examine the practices of individual enumerators in order to detect certain biases in their occupational reporting. On occasions the opinions of the enumerators shine through their returns. In Limehouse in 1871, for example, one enumerator described every prostitute as 'fallen' in the occupational column. The men in the brothels on census night were given such occupations as 'Gentleman (Query)', and 'Jack of all trades (Nothing)'. The enumerator added, 'These fallen women very often don't know either the names or ages of those men who slept with them, their ages are therefore only guessed at'.[2]

In broader terms, all occupations were also social designations reflecting status and perceived social worth. The differing assumptions which individual enumerators made about what constituted an occupation must be taken into consideration when analysing the data. In general terms, the full-time paid work of men creates few problems of interpretation. On the other hand, the recording of seasonal, casual or part-time labour is more problematic. This is especially true of the work of women and children, and in the

---

1   Office of Population Censuses and Surveys and the General Register Office, Edinburgh, *Guide to census reports*, pp 53–55.
2   RG 10/554, ff 116–118.

agricultural sector of the economy. The distinctions which were drawn between making and dealing, employers and employees, and those economically active and those unemployed and retired, are all obscure.

It is probable that the census authorities were not primarily concerned with gathering occupational data for economic analysis. They were most anxious to ensure that occupational terms were accompanied by the materials being worked upon; that people showed whether they were working with cotton, metals, animals, vegetable matter and so on. This in turn reflected a preoccupation with the effects of working with such materials on the character and life-expectancy of individuals. The medical aspects of the census, as noted in Chapter 2, should always be borne in mind.

The work of men

In general terms the paid employments of men appear to be fairly accurately recorded in the census returns. The evidence of occupations from nineteenth-century street directories appears in general to agree with that found in the census. Some occupations, such as bull-dog burner, doctor maker, keel bulley, sad-iron maker, tingle maker, and so on, may be difficult to interpret without the aid of a good occupational dictionary but such cases are generally few in number.

In other cases occupational terms may have more than one meaning, or a differing meaning in different parts of the country. A clothier in some parts meant a cloth maker, whereas elsewhere it meant a cloth dealer. A bricksetter in some areas meant a bricklayer, whilst in most areas it meant a man who performed certain operations in brickmaking. On the other hand, a bank manager might be the manager of a money bank but in mining districts the term could be used for someone who superintended operations at the pit head. An engineer might be a maker or driver of engines, or the term could be a shortened version of civil engineer. Such problems with local usages and double meanings are probably not too serious, however, when data is aggregated over large areas. In the case of local studies, however, an awareness of such linguistic variations is essential.

A more serious problem was the widespread tendency to omit the branch of employment or material being worked upon. Hence the appearance of undifferentiated terms such as 'labourer', 'weaver', 'spinner', and so on. The Census Office dealt with such vague terms in the process of abstracting data for the published tables by either creating vague headings such as 'Weaver (undefined)' and 'General labourer', or by assuming that they should be placed under the most common industry of the area.[3] Thus a 'weaver' might become a woollen weaver in Yorkshire, or a cotton weaver in Lancashire. These qualifying terms were sometimes added by the census clerks to the occupational descriptions in the enumerators' books.

---

3   RG 27/5, Item 69, p 4.

Multiple and seasonal occupations

In the nineteenth century work-patterns were more fluid than today. Even in the cities many people might have differing jobs according to the season of the year, whilst in the countryside the whole population might be called out to lend a hand at harvest time. An alternation between work on the land and at sea was the classic pattern for fishing communities in the period. A late example of this once more general seasonal pattern of labour can be found in the hop picking traditional amongst twentieth-century Londoners of the East End. People might also have complementary jobs such as butcher and grazier, or maltster and brewer.

The question of multiple occupations was covered in the householders' instructions from 1851 onwards.[4] In that year a person 'following more than one distinct trade may insert his occupations in the order of their importance'. The term 'distinct trade' became 'distinct business' in 1861, and 'distinct occupations' thereafter. Similarly, 'may' became 'should' in 1861, and 'must' from 1891 onwards. The masculine 'his' was dropped from the instructions in 1871. The tendency, therefore, was to strengthen the instruction whilst making it more generally applicable to the population. If large numbers of people, however, were not prepared to be specific about single occupations, one may have some doubts about the exhaustiveness of the recording of multiple occupations.

In the process of abstracting the data for publication the census clerks were instructed only to count the occupation which appeared 'most important', usually the first one given.[5] These occupations have sometimes been underlined by the clerks.

At the same time it must be remembered that tasks which are usually separated today into distinct occupations might be combined in the nineteenth century. Thus, a shoemaker might make shoes but could also sell them; a baker could make and also sell bread; and so on. It is probable that there was a gradual dissociation between making and selling in the period, and this may make the calculation of the numbers of those solely employed in retailing a difficult task.

There were no specific instructions given with regard to seasonal employments in the nineteenth-century censuses. In the case of women and children, their occupations were to be recorded if they were 'regularly employed from home'. But did this include harvest work, and what of the irregular tasks of the agricultural year, throwing stones at the crows, collecting windfalls, and the like? In general the returns give the impression that only the regular employments of men on census night were recorded. This is perhaps in keeping with the de facto nature of the census as a picture of society on one night every ten years. Since the census was usually taken in March or April, expressly in order to avoid the movements of the population during summer and the harvest season, part of the seasonal cycle of labour appears to be missing from the returns.

---

4   Examples of the household schedules can be found in various PRO record classes: 1841, RG 27/1, pp 56–57; 1851, HO 45/3579; 1861, RG 27/3, Item 2; 1871, RG 27/4, Item 5; 1881, RG 27/5, Item 5; 1891, RG 27/6, Item 68; 1901, RG 19/11.

5   RG 27/5, Item 69, p 2.

It is conceivable that the recording of such marginal occupations improved in 1891 because of the inclusion of questions on employment status. These may have encouraged a greater degree of care on the part of householders.

The work of women

There is a growing body of evidence which indicates problems with the recording of the work of women in the censuses. Women often worked on a casual, or part-time basis, and this labour frequently does not appear to have found its way into the returns as an 'occupation'. There are also the inevitable problems of how one treats the work of women in the home. Was such work an 'occupation', or 'merely' housework? This is especially serious when, as was very common in the nineteenth century, the home was a place of production of articles or services for sale, such as lodging houses, inns, farms, shops, and so on. The exact economic and social position of domestic servants also causes some problems.[6]

The domestic work of women in the family home was either directly or implicitly excluded from consideration in the census. In the examples provided on how to fill in the returns the occupational column for wives and daughters was left blank unless they had a specific paid occupation. From 1851 to 1881 a specific instruction was given that the 'occupations of women who are regularly employed from home, or at home, in any but domestic duties, [are] to be distinctly recorded'. However, the large number of female kin given occupational designations such as 'housekeeper', indicates that this distinction was not always finely drawn. In 1891, the general instruction was that, 'the occupations of women and children, if any, are to be stated as well as those of men'. In 1901 there was no instruction on the work of women at all.[7]

The work of women in the home which created services and products for sale was probably indifferently recorded. In 1841 this whole category of work was simply excluded by the instruction that, 'The profession &c of wives, or of sons or daughters living with and assisting their parents but not apprenticed or receiving wages, need not be inserted'.[8] The instruction of 1851 regarding women's work at home should have cleared up this problem but there is still some evidence that this was not regarded as an 'Occupation', and went unrecorded.

In the case of farms, however, the female kin of the householder were almost automatically assumed to be helping with agricultural tasks. In the years 1851 to 1881, the householders'

6   For a more general discussion of these problems see E Higgs, 'Women, occupations and work in the nineteenth century censuses', *History Workshop Journal*, XXIII (1987), pp 59–80; E Roberts, *Women's work 1840–1940* (London, 1988), pp 18–19.

7   Examples of the household schedules can be found in various PRO record classes: 1841, RG 27/1, pp 56–57; 1851, HO 45/3579; 1861, RG 27/3, Item 2; 1871, RG 27/4, Item 5; 1881, RG 27/5, Item 5; 1891, RG 27/6, Item 68; 1901, RG 19/11. Examples of the enumerators' books can be found in the relevant census classes for 1841 to 1881. Examples of those for 1891 can be found in RG 27/6, Items 71, 73, 74. The RG 27 volume for 1901 is 'Wanting' but the Office of Population Censuses and Surveys has supplied the author with a copy of the first five pages of an enumeration book. These contain printed pro forma material relating to fictitious persons rather than any information on named individuals.

8   RG 27/1, p 58.

examples showed the wife of the farmer described as a 'Farmer's wife'. In the same years, the householders were told that in the case of farmers, 'Sons or daughters employed at home or on the farm, may be returned – "Farmer's Son", "Farmer's Daughter" '. The instructions relating specifically to women on the farm were removed in 1891. These had previously caused confusion amongst some enumerators who described women as 'butcher's daughter', 'retired paper hanger's daughter', 'cotton spinner wife', and so on. The question arises as to whether these designations represent economically remunerative work, kin relationships, or multiple occupations (cotton spinner *and* wife?). There is even some evidence that the returns for women with permanent paid jobs in factories could be treated in the same manner or left blank. Could their domestic duties be seen as their proper occupation overriding paid work? In general, however, the recording of female factory workers appears to be fairly reliable.

These considerations should be born in mind when studying the employment of domestic servants, the largest category of employment for women in the period. In Rochdale in 1871 only one-third of the women described as being in servant occupations in the occupational column of the census were also described as servant in relationship to the head of the household. The majority of the remainder lived in the homes of their relatives. Many may have been day-servants or unemployed domestics living at home whilst they sought work but large numbers of 'housekeepers' and 'nurses' must have been performing 'domestic duties' at home.[9]

Still other servants worked on farms or in shops. The majority of servant employers in Rutland in 1871 were farmers, whilst retailers were always the largest category in mid-century Rochdale. It is conceivable that in many such households there was a strict demarcation between domestic, agricultural and retailing tasks but there is evidence that this was not the case in many small units of production.[10]

As with so many of the facets of census studies discussed here, it is essential to compare the conventions employed by neighbouring enumerators in order to understand their individual biases and styles. Some enumerators appear to have been less willing than others to regard the work of women as an 'Occupation'.

The work of children

The instructions in the censuses repecting the work of children were similar to those for women. Indeed, women and children were usually yoked together in the conventions to be used. The problems already noted regarding the enumeration of the work of women can also be found in the case of children.

9   For a more general discussion of the ambiguities relating to domestic service see E Higgs, 'The tabulation of occupations in the nineteenth-century census, with special reference to domestic servants', *Local Population Studies*, XXVIII (1982), pp 58–66; E Higgs, 'Domestic servants and households in Victorian England', *Social History*, VIII (1983), pp 201–210; E Higgs, 'Domestic service and household production', in *Unequal opportunities: women's employment in England 1800–1918*, ed. A V John (Oxford, 1986), pp 125–152; E Higgs, *Domestic servants and households in Rochdale, 1851–1871* (New York, 1986).
10   E Higgs, *Domestic servants and households in Rochdale*, pp 124–126; J A S Green, 'A survey of domestic service', *Lincolnshire History and Archaeology*, XVII (1982), pp 65–69; M Bouquet, *Family, servants and visitors: the farm household in nineteenth and twentieth century Devon* (Norwich, 1985), pp 75-79.

The family comprising an independent male 'breadwinner' with dependent wife and children was an ideal to which only certain sections of the population could aspire. The wages of men were often irregular, and illness and death could cause acute crises for working-class families. In these circumstances children were expected to make a contribution to the well-being of the family. This did not usually take the form of a full-time job but casual and part-time employment; looking after small children, running errands, foraging, helping in the family shop, or with the family laundry business, and so on. In the countryside children might be employed casually on such tasks as leading horses, weeding, bird scaring, and harvest work. The opportunities for such work differed, of course, from area to area and over time.[11]

There is some evidence that the census authorities understood this pattern of work. Even when the occupational column was left blank there are examples where boys aged ten to fourteen years have had the occupations of their fathers added by the census clerks in pencil. But, as in the case of women, such work was probably seldom seen as a formal 'Occupation'.

The most common designation for children in the census was that of 'scholar', and the censuses have been used by historians to calculate the number of children receiving education in the nineteenth century.[12] The returns should, however, be used with caution for this purpose. The definition of the term 'scholar' in the census instructions was vague, and became vaguer over time. With the advent of compulsory education after the 1870 Education Act there may also have been a temptation for some working-class householders to use the term to conceal the work of their children.

In 1851 parents were to record their children as 'scholars' if they were above five years of age and were 'daily attending school, or receiving regular tuition under a master or governess at home'. In 1861, however, regular tuition at home did not require the presence of a master or governess. In 1871 and 1881 children only needed to be 'attending a school, or receiving regular instruction at home', to be returned as scholars. In 1891 there was no instruction on the subject. In 1901, however, children attending school 'and also engaged in a trade or industry should be described as following the particular trade or industry'.[13]

Leaving aside the case of 1901, it would appear that the term 'scholar' became progressively less precise over time. How often or for what period of time should a scholar attend a school to be so defined? How did one define 'regular' tuition, and regular tuition in what? Did learning the family trade, or instruction in lacemaking at a 'lace-school' count? It was also possible, or at least consistent with the instructions, for a child who only attended Sunday school to be described as a 'scholar'.

The term was becoming increasingly vague at the very time when the pressures on the working classes to conceal the labour of their children was greatest. The Factory Acts of the

11   A Davin, 'Working or helping? London working-class children in the domestic economy', in *Households and the world economy*, eds J Smith, I Wallerstein, H Evers (London, 1984), pp 215–232.
12   See, for example, B I Coleman, 'The incidence of education in mid-century', in *Nineteenth-century society*, ed. Wrigley, pp 402–410.
13   Examples of the household schedules can be found in various PRO record classes: 1841, RG 27/1, pp 56–57; 1851, HO 45/3579; 1861, RG 27/3, Item 2; 1871, RG 27/4, Item 5; 1881, RG 27/5, Item 5; 1891, RG 27/6, Item 68; 1901, RG 19/11.

nineteenth century had placed some restrictions, which could be evaded, on the work of children under thirteen in factories. From 1870 onwards, however, various Education Acts still further curtailed the legal right of parents to dispose of their children's time, and a network of school attendance officers was established to ensure that children were sent to school. This was a double blow to working-class parents since they could no longer count upon the labour of their children to help supplement the family income, and they had to pay school fees as well. Although the latter could be remitted in cases of hardship, they were only abolished in the 1890s.[14]

In the first few decades of compulsory education the conflict between many working-class households and the school boards established to oversee the system was often severe. Truancy, often supported by parents, was common. Any enquiries in the census respecting the work of children might, therefore, be viewed with suspicion in working-class areas. This was certainly the view of witnesses before the 1890 Treasury Committee on the Census.[15] In London in 1871 they would have been justified in their suspicions since the census authorities broke their pledge of confidentiality and provided the London School Board with the names and addresses of all children aged between three and thirteen years, their exact ages, and the names and occupations of their parents.[16]

When the census totals of scholars are compared with contemporary surveys of schools certain anomalies become apparent. In 1851 the census enumerators left a separate educational schedule at every school of any description which they found in their district. The original schedules have not survived but printed summaries give the enrolment and attendance figures for male and female pupils at day schools and Sunday schools. This source gives a total of 1,139,300 boys enrolled at school in England and Wales, which compares almost exactly with the 1,148,100 male scholars in the census. On the other hand there were 1,096,000 female scholars in the latter but only 969,300 in the 1851 census of schools. The 1851 census did not cover every school, however, although the under-enumeration was probably quite small. At the same time the numbers actually attending school regularly would be less than those enrolled.[17]

A similar survey of schools was undertaken in 1871 and returns made of the number of children for whom accommodation in schools existed, and the number in attendance on the day the returns were made. The following table shows the returns for three civil parishes in Devon in which all schools made returns, and the numbers of scholars in these parishes in the 1871 census.[18]

14   P Horn, 'Child workers in the Victorian countryside: the case of Northamptonshire', *Northamptonshire Past and Present*, VII (1985–86), p 177.

15   *1890 report of the Treasury Committee on the Census*, QQ 821–823, 965, 1342.

16   *1890 report of the Treasury Committee on the Census*, QQ 2265–2266, 2480–2482; London School Board Statistical Committee (Greater London Record Office: SBL 908): SBL 908/Minutes of 3 April 1871, 15 May 1871 and 6 July 1871.

17   Coleman, 'The incidence of education in mid-century', p 403.

18   *Return relating to elementary education (civil parishes)*, PP 1871 LV [201], pp 72–73; Parish of Shute, RG 10/2035; Parish of Stockland, RG 10/2034; Parish of Uplyme, RG 10/2031.

Number of children for whom accommodation exists in schools	Number of children in attendance on day returns made		Number of census 'Scholars'	
	Male	Female	Male	Female
Parish of Shute 66	46	35	67	51
Parish of Stockland 146	63	63	83	69
Parish of Uplyme 94	31	23	76	74

Such returns are by no means conclusive proof of a general problem of over-enumeration of scholars in the population census but certainly point in that direction. The not uncommon cases of 'scholars' aged under five years of age should also indicate the problematic nature of the census data.

Even if children did attend schools, and were properly described as 'scholars', this did not necessarily mean that they did not perform some work. The imposition of compulsory education did not stop all remunerative work but probably displaced it into Saturday jobs and after school hours, with a resulting concentration in services and trading. Patterns of school attendances fitted into this regime of weekend or seasonal work, with high rates of absences on Mondays and Fridays, and at harvest time.[19]

Such problems may have declined in the later years of the century as children's labour came to be marginalised. This was due to the rise in the level of men's wages which cut down the need for a family contribution; the cumulative effects of factory and education legislation shortening the hours of work children could perform; the invention of the telephone which cut down the need for messengers; and above all, the decline of domestic industries such as lacemaking and shoemaking.[20]

Given these problems great care should be taken in using the census returns for calculating the provision of education in the period, and the participation rate of children in the economy. An examination of alternative sources, such as the surveys of schools, and a comparison of the conventions of neighbouring enumerators is of great importance. The temptation to regard all nineteenth-century children as unoccupied dependents should be avoided.

The agricultural workforce

The nineteenth century was a crucial period in the transition of England and Wales from a predominantly agricultural economy to a modern industrialised nation. In 1801 agriculture was the largest sector in the economy. One hundred years later the majority of people lived in towns, and the proportion of the population employed on the land was comparatively

19   Davin, 'Working or helping?', p 222; G Belfiore, 'Compulsion and community in the Essex textile districts', unpublished paper in the author's possession.
20   Davin, 'Working or helping?', p 226.

small. The census returns from 1841 onwards have been a principal source for the quantitative analysis of this decline.[21] There are problems with these returns, however, which must be borne in mind when attempting to calculate the size of the agricultural workforce.

The instructions for filling in the occupations of those working on farms changed over time.[22] In 1841 comparatively few instructions were given. The householder was told that, 'The profession &c of wives, or of sons and daughters living with and assisting their parents but not apprenticed or receiving wages, need not be inserted'. This immediately removed the work of the farmer's family from consideration. At the same time the enumerator was instructed that 'Ag. Lab.' was to be used as an abbreviation for agricultural labourer, 'which may include all farming servants and labourers in husbandry'.

In 1851 much more specific instructions were given. The householders were told that

> The term FARMER is to be applied only to the occupier of land, who is to be returned – "*Farmer of* [317] *acres employing* [12] *labourers*"; the number of acres, and of in and out-door labourers, on March 31st, being in all cases inserted. Sons or daughters employed at home or on the farm, may be returned – "*Farmer's son*", "*Farmer's daughter*".

The instructions to the enumerators repeated this guidance and added the following examples and notes:

> Farmer of 220 acres (employing 11 labourers).
> Bart; landed proprietor, farming 613 acres (employing 25 agricultural labourers).
> Farmer of 110 acres (employing 4 labourers and 1 boy).
> Farmer of 41 acres (employing 1 in and 1 out door labourer, with a boy).
> Freeholder, farmer of 10 acres (employing no labourer).
> Farmer's son (employed on the farm).
> Farmer's daughter (employed at home).
> The *acres* occupied by the farmer are to be stated exclusive of heath, mountain, moor, marsh, or common land – the extent of which used by the farmer should be *separately* stated. The number of *labourers* returned should include waggoners, shepherds, and

21   See, for example, C Booth, 'Occupations of the people of the United Kingdom, 1801–81', *Journal of the Statistical Society of London*, XLIX (1886), pp 314–444; B R Mitchell, *Abstract of British historical statistics* (Cambridge, 1962), pp 55–63; P Deane and W A Cole, *British economic growth, 1688–1959* (Cambridge, 1969), pp 136–173; W A Armstrong, 'The use of information about occupation. Part 2. An industrial classification, 1841–1891', in *Nineteenth-century society*, ed. Wrigley, pp 226–310; C H Feinstein, *National income, expenditure and output of the United Kingdom, 1855–1965* (Cambridge, 1972).

22   Examples of the household schedules can be found in various PRO record classes: 1841, RG 27/1, pp 56–57; 1851, HO 45/3579; 1861, RG 27/3, Item 2; 1871, RG 27/4, Item 5; 1881, RG 27/5, Item 5; 1891, RG 27/6, Item 68; 1901, RG 19/11. Examples of the enumerators' books can be found in the relevant census classes for 1841 to 1881. Examples of those for 1891 can be found in RG 27/6, Items 71, 73, 74. The RG 27 volume for 1901 is 'Wanting' but the Office of Population Censuses and Surveys has supplied the author with a copy of the first five pages of an enumeration book. These contain printed pro forma material relating to fictitious persons rather than any information on named individuals.

all kinds of workmen employed on the farm, whether they sleep in the house or not; and when *boys* or women are employed, their number should be separately given. The male and female farm servants who sleep in house will be entered in the household schedule, and their particular employments, as waggoner, dairy maid, &c., inserted in the column headed "Occupation".

These rather complex instructions plainly prescribed an exhaustive itemised description of the resources of the farm. In practice, however, the precise definitions of the acreage and numbers of labourers to be returned appear to have been lost on most farmers and enumerators.

The instructions in 1861 were much less detailed. The householder was told that

> The term FARMER to be applied only to the OCCUPIER of land. Example: *"Farmer of 317 acres, employing 8 labourers and 3 boys"*; the actual number of acres, and of men and boys employed on the farm, on April 8th, being in all cases inserted. Sons or daughters employed at home or on the farm, may be returned – *"Farmer's son"*, *"Farmer's daughter"*.

> FARM SERVANTS sleeping in the Farmer's house must be described in his schedule as *"Carter"*, *"Dairymaid"*, &c., as the case may be.

> An out-door LABOURER working on a farm must be described as *"Agricultural labourer"*; *"Shepherd"*, &c., as the case may be.

The 1851 instructions on the type of land to be included in the acreage were dropped. At the same time the number of women working on the farm was not mentioned.

In 1871 and 1881 the number of men, women and boys working on the farm was supposed to be returned. But only men employed on the farms and sleeping in the farmer's house were to be described as farm servants. This gradual exclusion of women was taken a stage further in 1891 when householders were instructed to return only 'SONS or other RELATIVES of FARMERS employed on the farm . . . as *"Farmer's son"*, *"Farmer's brother"*.' The daughters of farmers were no longer mentioned.

The other important change in 1891 was the abandonment of any returns on the acreage of farms and the numbers of labourers employed. This was the first census at which people were asked to state whether they were employers or employees, and it may have been considered that a specific question regarding employment on farms was now redundant.

There are plainly some problems with these returns. First, the under-enumeration of seasonal and casual work, and of the work of women and children, is probably most serious with respect to agricultural employment. As mentioned above, the exact status of female servants on the farm is especially difficult to determine. Were they domestic or agricultural workers? Such problems may be more serious in the north and west where the predominance of dairy farming provided a demand for casual and seasonal female labour. In the arable east and south the participation of women in field work was less.[23] The instructions given failed to define the term 'Farmer', and there was plainly confusion as to what was to be returned under acreage and the numbers employed.

---

23   K D M Snell, 'Agricultural seasonal employment, the standard of living, and women's work in the south and east, 1690–1860', *Economic History Review*, 2nd Series, XXXIV (1981), pp 407–437.

Since no lower limit was placed on the size of a holding which could be termed a farm, 'farmers' occupying one or two acres can be found. The distinction between such 'farmers' and market gardeners is plainly difficult to draw. Some people combining farming as a subsidiary trade with some other occupation, such as miller, baker, publican, and even labourer, recorded themselves as occupying larger acreages. The division between agricultural and non-agricultural employment was often ill defined. Still other 'farmers' neglected to give any acreage returns at all. Some of these will, no doubt, have been retired from the land. One nineteenth-century study claimed that retired farmers were no more than two per cent of the total, although another contemporary study of Huntingdon put the figure nearer twelve per cent.[24]

When the acreage returns in the census have been checked against other contemporary sources, such as tithe apportionments and parish rate books, a fair degree of consistency appears to emerge.[25] It should be noted, however, that the returns for 1851 were supposed to differentiate between land in and out of agricultural use, whilst the instructions for later years could be taken as referring to total acreage. The extent to which this created confusion, especially in 1851, is difficult to determine.

The returns for the numbers of persons employed on the farm are extremely problematic. In theory farmers were to give the total number of people working on the farm irrespective of whether they were living-in farm servants, agricultural labourers who lived out, women or children. Women, however, appear to have been excluded in 1861. Some farmers neglected to make any returns under this head at all, and it cannot be assumed that they did so because they did not employ anyone. The number of women and children employed, moreover, often seems to have been left out. It is also difficult to decide what the number of agricultural labourers in the returns refers to.

Agricultural historians who have studied the returns have concluded that only the number of agricultural labourers employed by the farmer but not living in his or her house were returned. Farm servants living on the farm are supposed to have been excluded.[26] But this perhaps draws too much of a distinction between the two terms. In 1841 the term 'agricultural labourer' was expressly to be used for 'all farming servants and labourers in husbandry'. In 1851 the enumerators were told that the number of labourers was to include all 'workmen employed on the farm, whether they sleep in the house or not'. In 1861 'labourers' appears only to have related to men and boys; women were not mentioned. Thereafter the term was to apply to the total number of men, women and boys employed on the farm. One cannot assume, therefore, that the bald statement 'Farmer X employs 3 labourers', relates to only one category of employees.

Adding up the number of persons employed by farmers in a particular parish or township, and comparing this to the number of persons in agricultural occupations in the same area

24   D Grigg, 'Farm size in England and Wales, from early Victorian times to the present', *Agricultural History Review*, XXXV (1987), p 181.
25   S Thomas, 'The enumerators' returns as a source for a period picture of the parish of Llansantffraid, 1841–1851', *Ceredigion*, IV (1963), p 409; S Thomas, 'The agricultural labour force in some south-west Carmarthenshire parishes in the mid-nineteenth century', *Welsh History Review*, III (1966–67), p 64.
26   J A Sheppard, 'The east Yorkshire agricultural labour force in the mid-nineteenth century', *Agricultural History Review*, IX (1961), p 45; Thomas, 'The agricultural labour force in some south-west Carmarthenshire parishes', p 67.

is not always a meaningful exercise.[27] The two figures might not be even approximately similar if large numbers of agricultural labourers lived in one parish but worked in another. Female farm servants may well not be included in the number of labourers employed, and this might explain why in some cases the total number of farm servants in an area exceeds the figure for the number of persons employed. Such analyses on a county-wide basis are perhaps less prone to such errors.

It is very difficult, therefore, to say exactly what the returns refer to, and this presumably depended on the interpretation put on the complicated instructions by farmers and enumerators. As ever, a careful scrutiny of the returns for local and personal idiosyncracies is extremely important.

An additional problem was the tendency of householders and enumerators to describe people as 'labourers' without indicating if they were agricultural workers, casual dock labourers, road workers, and so on. In thoroughly rural areas one might be justified in assuming these to be agricultural labourers but there will be problems in doing so elsewhere. The GRO got over this problem by placing all such persons in a vague residual category for 'General labourers'.[28] The published tables in the *Census reports* therefore underestimate the size of the agricultural workforce.

Undoubtedly the returns of the agricultural workforce can be used for very broad regional comparisons but their use in local studies is fraught with dangers.

Employers and employees

The GRO was interested in distinguishing between employers and employees from the very first census under its control. Its efforts in this respect do not appear to have borne fruit, however, and this can be explained, in part, by the difficulties inherent in trying to pin down fluid nineteenth-century employment practices. The instructions also show a gradual progression from a model of the economy based on the old handicraft distinctions between 'master', 'apprentice', and 'journeyman', to one structured around the polarity of 'employer' and 'worker'.[29]

The distinction to be made in 1841 was essentially a negative one. Enumerators were told to put down people's employments,

> writing "*J.*" for *Journeyman*, "*Ap.*" for *Apprentice*, and "*Sh.*" for *Shopman*, after the statement of the trade of those who are such. "*Master*" need not be inserted; every one will be so considered who is not entered as journeyman or apprentice.

---

27   C Thomas, 'Rural society in nineteenth-century Wales: south Cardiganshire in 1851', *Ceredigion*, VI (1970), pp 397–398; S Thomas, 'The enumerators' returns as a source for a period picture', pp 412–413.

28   RG 27/5, Item 69, p 4; RG 27/6, Item 61, p 4.

29   Examples of the household schedules can be found in various PRO record classes: 1841, RG 27/1, pp 56–57; 1851, HO 45/3579; 1861, RG 27/3, Item 2; 1871, RG 27/4, Item 5; 1881, RG 27/5, Item 5; 1891, RG 27/6, Item 68; 1901, RG 19/11. Examples of the enumerators' books can be found in the relevant census classes for 1841 to 1881. Examples of those for 1891 can be found in RG 27/6, Items 71, 73, 74. The RG 27 volume for 1901 is 'Wanting' but the Office of Population Censuses and Surveys has supplied the author with a copy of the first five pages of an enumeration book. These contain printed pro forma material relating to fictitious persons rather than any information on named individuals.

Comparatively few people followed this instruction and so the exact distinction between master, apprentice and day labourer was obscured.

In 1851 fuller instructions were provided for the enumerators:

> In TRADES the master is to be distinguished from the Journeyman and Apprentice, thus – "(*Carpenter, master employing [6] men*)"; inserting always the number of persons of the trade in his employment on March 31st.

> Baker (master employing 4 men, 2 women).
> Bootmaker (journeyman).
> Ironmonger's apprentice.
> Shoemaker (master employing 15 men, 3 women).

> In trades where women or boys and girls are employed, the number of each class should be separately given. Where the master is one of a manufacturing or mercantile firm, the entry should be after this form: – "Cotton manufacturer – firm of 3, employ 512 men, 273 women, 35 boys, and 272 girls."

On the other hand, shareholders in companies and the owners of mines were not to return themselves as employers but as 'Fund-holder', 'Proprietor of iron mines', and so on.

In the 1861 instructions to the householders the master was defined in terms of being an employer:

> IN TRADES, MANUFACTURES, or other business, the employer must, in all cases, be distinguished; Example: "*Carpenter-master, employing 6 men and 2 boys*"; inserting always the number of persons of the trade in his employ, if any, on April 8th.

Fund-holders and the proprietors of mines were to be treated as in 1851. In the case of firms, however, the number of persons employed only needed to be returned by one partner. In 1871 and 1881 the instructions reverted to talking of a 'Master' as opposed to an 'Employer', and in the case of firms the numbers employed were to be returned by 'the senior or some one partner only'. In these years those deriving their income from dividends were to describe themselves as such but nothing specific was said about mine owners.

In 1891 the system was radically changed by the introduction of three columns for employment status. These were headed 'Employer', 'Employed', and 'Neither employer nor employed, but working on own account'. An 'Employer' was defined as 'a master, employing under him workers in his trade or industry'. A cross was to be placed in the relevant column. Married women assisting their husbands in their trade were to be returned as 'Employed'.

The occupation column was retained, however, and the enumerators' instructions still showed the terms 'Master' and 'Apprentice' being added to occupations. Those owning shares in companies were now to describe themselves as 'Living on their own means'. The growing complexity of employer/employee relations was recognised by the inclusion of instructions regarding managers, foremen and superintendents.

In 1901 only one extra column was used, in which householders were now to write 'Employer', 'Worker' or 'Own Account'. The employment of domestic servants was not to be counted. The examples of the occupational column no longer mentioned masters or apprentices. There was also no specific mention of fund-holders but those 'deriving their income from private sources should return themselves as "Living on own means"'.

Despite all these elaborate instructions the returns under this head were plainly imperfect. In the years 1851 to 1881 many employers failed to indicate the number of persons they employed, although in some cases this may reflect the fact that householders were following the instructions relating to partnerships. Even fewer people took the trouble to describe themselves as an 'apprentice' or a 'journeyman', and these terms must have become increasingly obsolete in many industries. In 1891 the census authorities expressed themselves bitterly disappointed by the entries in the three employment status columns. People put crosses in more than one column, and it was felt that many had inflated their social position by putting a cross under the heading 'Employer'.[30]

These latter problems may, however, have been exaggerated by the census authorities. There may have been perfectly good reasons why householders placed crosses in more than one column. People with more than one occupation, e.g. 'Farmer and agricultural labourer', might be employed in one and self-employed in another. Others may have worked in trades such as building where subcontracting was widespread. A person might be employed to complete a job, and then employ others to do the work. Those in managerial roles might be the employees of a company but employ others on behalf of the firm. Even workers in the lowest social classes might be employers. Costermongers, for example, might employ children for a few pence, or for as much fruit as they could eat, to mind the stall.[31]

The GRO had also been forced against its will to introduce the three columns by the 1890 Treasury Committee on the Census, and may have been unnecessarily critical of the results as a consequence.[32] Such 'problems' may have been overcome in 1901, when only one column was available for such information, but this does not necessarily mean that the data supplied was nearer to economic reality.

Retirement and unemployment

Similar difficulties are to be found in relation to the information on retirement and unemployment in the census schedules. The GRO wished to know the former occupations of people in such circumstances in order to calculate occupational life tables for actuarial purposes. The problems which arose reflected, no doubt, the difficulties of defining these terms in the nineteenth-century context, and of the changing instructions in the schedules themselves. It is therefore difficult to estimate the proportion of the population which fell into these categories. It is interesting, however, that the category in the 1831 census for

30   *1891 census report*, p 36.
31   The author is grateful to Kevin Schurer of the Cambridge Group for the History of Population and Social Structure for these comments.
32   Higgs, 'The struggle for the occupational census', pp 81–86.

those who were retired or disabled comprised nearly six per cent of all males over twenty.[33]

In 1841 neither state was mentioned but in 1851 householders were instructed that

> Persons of advanced age who have RETIRED FROM BUSINESS to be entered thus –"Retired Silk Merchant", "Retired Watchmaker", &c.

> ALMSPEOPLE, and persons in the receipt of parish relief should, after being described as such have their previous occupations inserted.

The instruction in 1861 was similar, although the clause 'of advanced aged' had been dropped. Rather confusingly, however, the example on the schedule showed a woman described as 'Formerly Laundress'.

In 1871 and 1881 the householders' instructions dropped any specific mention of almspeople, whilst retaining the wording of the 1861 instructions as to the retired. Unemployment made its first specific appearance in these years with the instruction that, 'Persons ordinarily engaged in some industry, but OUT OF EMPLOYMENT on April 2nd, should be so described, as *"Coal miner, unemployed"*, *"Printer, unemployed"*.' Some inconsistency crept in, however, since the example on the enumerators' schedule contained the entry, 'Ship carpenter (out of employ)'.

In 1891 and 1901, with the introduction of the columns for employment status, the question regarding unemployment was dropped. The guidance regarding retirement was broadened, however, with the instruction that, 'Persons who have *retired* from their profession, business, or occupation must state their former calling with the addition of the word "Retired" '. The household schedule now contained a 'Retired Laundress' in its example.

The returns under these headings were plainly imperfect. Information on unemployment was seldom given. The inmates of prisons, hospitals and workhouses often have specific occupations against their names, although they might more properly be regarded as retired or unemployed. People are sometimes described as 'annuitants' (the term could refer to someone receiving an annual allowance, as well as to a person with an investment producing an annual return), although they were probably institutionalised pensioners. Many very elderly people have no occupation recorded at all, although we might regard them as having been retired. The list of such ambiguities could be multiplied.

Part of the problem may have been the difficulty in making a definite distinction between being in employment, and being retired or unemployed. When work was very casual and stoppages frequent, especially in the last years of people's working lives, the distinction

33   Examples of the household schedules can be found in various PRO record classes: 1841, RG 27/1, pp 56–57; 1851, HO 45/3579; 1861, RG 27/3, Item 2; 1871, RG 27/4, Item 5; 1881, RG 27/5, Item 5; 1891, RG 27/6, Item 68; 1901, RG 19/11. Examples of the enumerators' books can be found in the relevant census classes for 1841 to 1881. Examples of those for 1891 can be found in RG 27/6, Items 71, 73, 74. The RG 27 volume for 1901 is 'Wanting' but the Office of Population Censuses and Surveys has supplied the author with a copy of the first five pages of an enumeration book. These contain printed pro forma material relating to fictitious persons rather than any information on named individuals. E A Wrigley, 'Men on the land and men in the countryside: employment in agriculture in early-nineteenth-century England', in *The world we have gained. Histories of population and social structure*, eds L Bonfield, R M Smith and K Wrightson (Oxford, 1986), p 306.

might be very difficult to draw. A dock labourer, for example, might not know if he was to get work until he turned up at the dock gates in the morning. On the other hand, someone in business or a farmer might have handed over control of the business for all practical purposes to a son, and yet still have regarded himself or herself as the titular head of the firm or farm. Similarly, despite the introduction of the new poor law in the 1830s, many paupers receiving out-relief still had some employment. Hence entries such as 'in receipt of parish relief and straw-bonnet maker', or 'pauper and charwoman', or 'Carpenter (parish pay)'.

The returns under these headings must, therefore, be used with caution. Certainly some common-sense rules have to be applied to the inmates of institutions, who cannot be regarded as part of the economically active population. The problem is, of course, to decide which of the inmates were temporarily out of the labour market, and which were permanently institutionalised. In later years the GRO's own solution was to regard everyone sixty years and over as having retired but to count the rest as having an occupation.[34]

Working at home

In 1901 another column was added for home working. The instruction at the head of the column read, 'Write opposite the name of each person carrying on trade or industry at home the words "At home"'.[35] This instruction appears rather vague; did it include servants or housewives? The census authorities do not appear to have used this information in their tabulations, and did not comment on the accuracy of the data.

Socio-economic groupings and life-cycle stages

Historians and sociologists have used the occupational data in the censuses to construct various measurements of the status and welfare of households. Such methods of grouping households are necessary prerequisites for the aggregate analysis of census populations. Leaving aside the general question of what exactly one means by social 'status', there are some practical problems with using census data in this manner which can be mentioned here. This is not to dissuade historians from using such techniques but merely to point out some of their limitations.

Socio-economic groupings are based upon the principle that nineteenth-century census households can be assigned to specific social strata or classes according to the occupation of the head. Following the work of Armstrong on the 1841 and 1851 censuses, the most frequently used schema for such assignments is that drawn up by the General Register Office for use in the census of 1951.[36] By the use of occupational dictionaries each occupation can be assigned to one of five classes:

34   RG 27/6, Item 61, p 2.
35   RG 19/11.
36   Armstrong, 'The use of information about occupation', pp 198–225; A Armstrong, *Stability and change in an English county town. A social study of York 1801–51* (London, 1974), pp 13–15.

Class I   Professional, etc., occupations
Class II   Intermediate occupations
Class III Skilled occupations
Class IV Partly skilled occupations
Class V   Unskilled occupations

An accountant, and his family, would be placed in Class I, and a road labourer in Class V.

Armstrong modified the 1951 attribution lists in the following manner for use with the 1851 census data:

1   all employers of twenty-five or more persons were raised to Class I, whatever their classification in the registrar general's 1951 lists;
2   all 'dealers', 'merchants', except those distinctly described as brokers or agents (Class II) or hawkers (Class V), and all persons engaged in retail board, lodging and catering were initially classed as III, despite the fact that the registrar general's list placed them variously;
3   from Class III (or in a few cases IV), upon consideration of individual cases, those who employed at least one person, other than their own family, were then raised to Class II. In boarding, catering, etc., the employment of one or more servants was taken to count for this purpose;
4   house and land proprietors, those 'living off interest' or 'of independent means', annuitants and paupers were placed in Classes I, I, I, II, and V respectively;
5   uninformative entries such as 'husband away', or 'spinster' were placed in a residual Class X, and retired persons were classified on the basis of their previous occupations.

Armstrong had to modify his schema still further for the analysis of the 1841 census because at that date individuals were not asked to state whether or not they were employers, or their number of employees. He again used the 1951 attributions as his point of departure but used the following modifications:

Class I – as in 1851, less unidentified large entrepreneurs;
Class II – individuals who would have been assigned to Classes II and III according to the 1851 procedures, provided they employed at least one servant;
Class III – the same, where no servants were employed;
Classes IV and V – according to the initial attribution list.

This schema has been criticised on the grounds that it is inappropriate to use a twentieth-century social classification to order nineteenth-century data. The Armstrong classification also assigns a very large number of households to Class III.[37] Armstrong also depends upon information on the employment of servants to assign households to socio-economic groups. As was noted above, however, the exact employment status of 'servants' can be obscure. In 1841 there was no column for relationship to head, so there is no way of telling if a person with a servant occupation was in service in the household in which they resided. They may have been day or unemployed servants living with relatives or in lodgings.

37   Armstrong, *Stability and change*, p 15.

There are also problems over the use of the number of hands employed. Some employers neglected to give this information, and they would have been perfectly correct to do so from 1861 onwards if they were one of the partners in a firm. The Armstrong system breaks down after 1881 because in 1891 and 1901 employers were not required to state the number of hands they employed. The classification can only be used with any degree of confidence for the thirty year period 1851 to 1881.

Armstrong 'proves' the validity of his schema, in part, by showing that the employment of servants was greater on average the higher one goes up his social scale.[38] But this is a circular argument because he uses the employment of servants to assign households to his higher social categories. The relationship between servant employment and social status is also not so clear cut as one might assume.[39] Some of these problems might be overcome if one could link census data to other sources, those indicating the rent levels or rateable values of accommodation for example.

Another problem with such socio-economic classification systems is that they assign households to status groups according to the occupation of the, usually male, household head. Amongst the working classes, however, prosperity was often determined by the total family income, including that brought in by wives and children, and the total number of mouths to be fed. This has led some historians to group households for the purposes of analysis in life-cycle stages according to the relative number of children in and out of employment. A working-class household with a large number of children not at work is assumed to be in more difficult financial circumstances than one without children, or children at work. The use of such classifications for the analysis of nineteenth-century census data was pioneered by Anderson,[40] who distinguished, for married couples only, the following stages:

1 Wife under forty-five, no children at home.
2 Wife under forty-five, one child under one year old at home.
3 Children at home, but none in employment.
4 Children at home, and some, but under half, in employment.
5 Children at home, and half, or over half, in employment.
6 Wife forty-five and over, no children, or one only over twenty, at home.

The analysis of households arranged in this schema is a much more subtle use of sociological methodology. There are still problems, however, with the construction of such groupings. The work of women is obscured in this classification, and it is dependent upon the employment of children being consistently given. As was noted above, this is just the sort of occupational data which the census often lacks. At best life-cycle stages, as well as socio-economic groupings, must be regarded as crude analytical tools.

38   Armstrong, 'The use of information about occupation', pp 211–212.
39   Higgs, *Domestic servants and households in Rochdale*, pp 102–109.
40   M Anderson, *Family structure in nineteenth century Lancashire* (London, 1971), p 202.

Abbreviations

In the course of copying out their returns, the enumerators were given permission to use certain abbreviations for occupations.[41] This practice was most extensive in 1841, and gradually diminished thereafter. By 1871 the only abbreviation mentioned was 'Ag. Lab.' for agricultural labourer. In 1881 a more general instruction was given:

> such contractions may be used as "ag. lab." for agricultural labourer, but care must be taken that the contractions used are such as will be readily understood.

From 1891 onwards no mention was made of the possibility of using such abbreviations.

The following table contains the abbreviations mentioned in the instructions on the enumeration schedules:

Abbreviation	Date	Meaning
Ag. Lab.	1841–1881	Agricultural labourer
Ap.	1841–1861	Apprentice
Army	1841	Members of HM land forces of whatever rank
Cl.	1841–1861	Clerk
F.S.	1841	Female servant
H.P.	1841	Members of HM armed forces on half pay
Ind.	1841	Independent-people living on their own means
J.	1841	Journeyman
M.	1841	Manufacturer
m.	1841	Maker–as in 'Shoe m.'
M.S.	1841	Male servant
Navy	1841	Members of HM naval forces, including marines, of whatever rank
P.	1841	Pensioners in HM armed forces
Rail. Lab.	1851	Railway labourer
Serv.	1861	Servant
Sh.	1841	Shopman

41   Examples of the household schedules can be found in various PRO record classes: 1841, RG 27/1, pp 56–57; 1851, HO 45/3579; 1861, RG 27/3, Item 2; 1871, RG 27/4, Item 5; 1881, RG 27/5, Item 5; 1891, RG 27/6, Item 68; 1901, RG 19/11. Examples of the enumerators' books can be found in the relevant census classes for 1841 to 1881. Examples of those for 1891 can be found in RG 27/6, Items 71, 73, 74. The RG 27 volume for 1901 is 'Wanting' but the Office of Population Censuses and Surveys has supplied the author with a copy of the first five pages of an enumeration book. These contain printed pro forma material relating to fictitious persons rather than any information on named individuals.

Part IV   References and finding-aids

12 References and finding-aids

It is not the purpose of this chapter to give a detailed account of the way in which one can find a place or person in the census returns. Microfilm copies of the censuses can be found in numerous local record offices and libraries, as well as at the PRO, and it would be impossible to describe all the differing finding-aids in use. A considerable amount of work is also going on in record offices, libraries, and family history societies to produce new and improved indexes and guides. A description of the finding-aids extant at any one point in time would, therefore, very quickly become outdated.

All that will be attempted here is to describe the reference system used at the PRO which enables one to give a unique reference to every page in the census returns, and to give a general outline of the types of finding aids available at the PRO and in local repositories. Some general guidance on the conventions for producing these will also be provided.

Where to find the census returns

The original census returns for the period 1841 to 1881 are currently held in the PRO's repository in Hayes, Middlesex. These are not made available to the public except in very special circumstances, and one has to use the microfilm copies currently housed in the PRO's Portugal Street and Chancery Lane offices. The census records are so heavily used that the originals would soon be destroyed if members of the public were allowed to consult them directly. The censuses are currently made available to the public when they are 100 years old. This means that the 1891 census will be open for inspection in January 1992.

The pre–1841 nominal returns were probably only created in certain areas, and were unlikely to have been sent to the central authorities. Some appear to have been preserved by the local poor law officers and clergy who produced them, and found their way into local poor law records and parish chests. In many cases these records have subsequently been deposited in local record offices and libraries, although others may still remain with the parish authorities.

The most comprehensive topographical listing of these returns can be found in the journal *Local Population Studies*.[1] This indicates the existence of a copy of these returns held by the Cambridge Group for the History of Population and Social Structure[2] and gives some indication of the information they contain. Unfortunately, the listings do not give the addresses of the repositories where the originals can be found. The Cambridge Group is a research unit for the study of historical demography, and is very helpful in supplying information to academic and amateur historians but it does not have the resources to act as an archive in its own right. Recourse to it for information should be undertaken only as a last resort. References to many of these returns can also be found in Jeremy Gibson's *Census returns on microfilm 1841–1881*.[3]

1   *Local Population Studies*, XXIV (1980)–XXXVII (1986).
2   27 Trumpington Street, Cambridge, CB2 1QA.
3   J Gibson, *Census returns on microfilm, 1841–1881. A directory to local holdings* (Plymouth, 1982). This can be obtained from the Federation of Family History Societies, or from Mr Gibson direct (Harts Cottage, Church Hanborough, Oxford, OX7 2AB).

The latter work is mainly dedicated to indicating where local copies of the post–1831 census microfilms can be found. Many local record offices and local history libraries have now purchased copies of these returns. It should be noted, however, that these local repositories usually only acquire the returns for the administrative areas within which they lie. It should also be noted that these modern administrative areas are usually different from the old historical counties of the nineteenth century. The collection in a local repository may also not include the microfilms for every year. Having located a likely repository it is always advisable to check with them about their holdings before going to consult the returns. The Genealogical Society of Utah also lends microfilm of the returns through their branch library system.

The records of the 1891 and 1901 censuses are in the custody of the Office of Population Censuses and Surveys (OPCS), and direct descendants of people appearing in them can obtain the age and place of birth of named persons from the returns on payment of a fee. Applications should be made to the General Register Office (now part of OPCS), Room 115, St Catherine's House, Kingsway, London, WC2B 6JP.

PRO references

Most people will, at one time or another, have used the index in a book to find information. In a book such an index refers to subjects, persons or places arranged in alphabetical order, and gives page references. The pages in the book will be conveniently numbered 1, 2, 3 . . ., and so on, for this purpose. The page number acts as a reference. An archive, such as the PRO, can be seen as a vast reference book but with a much more complicated system of references. Since the records all fall into differing series which have to be kept distinct, and each series has its own internal structure, references to consecutively numbered pages cannot be used. It is still necessary, however, to have some system which uniquely identifies each piece of information in the archive.

Public records usually take the form of a series of like records produced for a common purpose; a series of letter books, a file series, a set of census returns, and so on. Such series are usually designated as classes within the PRO and have a class code made up of a letter code and a number. HO 45, for example, is the main registered file series in the Home Office, whilst RG 18 is a series of maps showing the boundaries of registration districts in the nineteenth, and early twentieth, centuries. The following list gives the PRO class references for the census returns from 1841 to 1901:

Class Reference	Years
HO 107	1841 & 1851
RG 9	1861
RG 10	1871
RG 11	1881
RG 12*	1891
RG 13*	1901

*Currently closed to public inspection.

Every class is made up of a number of pieces, each piece being a single orderable item within the record office. Each piece has a reference made up of the class reference, a slash, and usually a number. The first orderable unit in the 1861 census returns is thus RG 9/1. It should be noted that a piece reference does not necessarily refer to a single artefact, it may relate to a bundle of letters, a box of miscellaneous papers, a sack of rolls, and so on. It is basically only a stock control reference.

Within the piece the structure of the records will define the internal system of references used. A single volume may have page numbers; the letters within a file may be referred to by the names of the correspondents and the date; each of the papers in a box may have a registered number which forms their references within the piece; and so on.

The structure of the various sets of census returns varies, and so do the reference systems used to identify pieces of information within them. The records for each census are arranged in the topographical order outlined in Chapter 6. This means that the 1841 records are in a very different order from those produced later, since they are mainly arranged according to hundreds and parishes rather than by registration districts. But the main difference in the reference systems lies in the manner in which the returns have subsequently been boxed and numbered.

In the 1841 records each piece is a box containing folders. Each piece contains the folders covering a hundred or the parishes forming part of a hundred, and has a reference such as HO 107/1. Each folder in turn contains several enumerators' books, and has the numbers of the enumeration districts these cover on the front. Each folder has a reference dependent upon its position within the piece. The first folder in the box is number 1, the second is number 2, and so on. Each folder is therefore identified by the piece number and this subnumber, in the form HO 107/1/1 or HO 107/670/2. On the microfilm copies of these records, these references appear on each frame of the film. Part of this extended reference can be found on the bottom on the folder covers in the form $^{670}/_2$. To complicate matters somewhat the PRO has traditionally called each folder an 'enumeration book', and each enumerator's book an 'enumeration district'.

Within each folder, or 'enumeration book', each folio is numbered from one to x in the top right hand corner from the front cover to the end of the folder. This means that a single enumerator's book may cover folios thirty-eight to fifty-six within a folder. The enumerators' books have their own internal numbering system, of course, with the pages for nominal information numbered one to x. This means that the exact reference for each page of the 1841 returns is made up of five pieces of information; the class code, the piece number, the book (i.e. folder) number, the folio number, and the page number, e.g. HO 107/504, bk 9, f 5, p 2.

In the case of the 1851 returns, each piece is again a box containing folders. Each piece usually covers a registration district or a number of subdistricts forming part of one. The returns continue the piece numbering of the 1841 series, so the first piece number for the 1851 returns is HO 107/1466. This number is, as before, on each frame of the microfilm copies. Each folder, again called an 'enumeration book' at the PRO, contains a number of enumerators' books.

The contents of each piece are again foliated. But whereas in 1841 each folder was separately foliated, in 1851 the piece was foliated as a whole, starting with the first folio of the first enumerator's book in the first folder, and ending with the last folio in the last enumerator's book in the last folder. One folder may have the reference HO 107/1698, ff 161–394, and an enumerator's book within it the reference HO 107/1698, ff 205–230.

Each enumerator's book has its district number in the top right hand corner of the front page, and its own internal pagination. Each page in the 1851 returns, therefore, has a reference such as HO 107/1798, f 52, p 4, made up of four elements; the class number, the piece number, the folio number, and the page number.

In the period 1861 to 1881, each piece is the folder containing a number of enumerators' books. The piece usually covers the whole or part of a sub-district rather than a district. Each set of returns forms a separate class, with pieces numbered one to x. The first folder in the 1881 returns is therefore RG 11/1. Again, the folder is referred to as an 'enumeration book' at the PRO.

Each piece, or folder, is foliated from the first folio in the first enumerator's book to the last folio in the last enumerator's book. An enumerator's book could, therefore, cover folios fifteen to thirty-eight within the piece. Each enumerator's book has its district number at the top right hand corner of the front page, and its own internal pagination. Each page in the returns, therefore, has a reference in the form RG 9/38, f 18, p 3. The returns for 1891 and 1901 are not yet available for inspection but will probably follow the same reference system.

The reference system used at the PRO uniquely identifies each page in the returns, and should always be used when referring to census data. It should be noted, however, that it refers solely to the actual manuscripts, and has nothing to do with the microfilm copies which most people use. Each reel of microfilm may contain copies of several pieces, and even parts of pieces, although the extent of the latter can still be deduced from the PRO foliation on the film.

Finding a place or address

Since the census returns are arranged topographically, generally in the order places appear in the published population tables, the finding aids at the PRO are similarly arranged. They are laid out by parishes, hundreds, or registration districts. To use the census returns it is necessary to have some geographical information; the name of a street, parish, township, and so on. People with the name Smith are not, of course, grouped together, nor is it easy to directly identify areas which are meaningful in a sociological sense, such as those occupied by distinct social groups.

At the PRO the finding-aids for the censuses of 1841, 1851 and 1861 are currently marked up copies of the published population tables. Those for later censuses are typed lists but still follow the order and layout of the published tables. In order to find the piece reference for the returns covering a particular place, it is necessary to use special placename indexes to find the page of the 1841 list, or, for later censuses, the number of the registration sub-district, in which they can be found. There are different indexes for each census. One can then go to the marked up tables, or the class lists, to find the relevant entry. The places within a particular hundred or registration district will be given, broadly in the order in which they appear in the returns. To the side of the entry will be a reference to the appropriate PRO piece number which one uses to order the microfilm of the record.

An example may help to elucidate this procedure. The 1871 placename index indicates that the parish of Friston in Suffolk then lay in the registration district of Plomesgate (district number 215), in sub-district 5. The number of the registration sub-district was therefore 215:5. If one goes to the RG 10 list, one can look up the 215th district, and the fifth sub-district within it. This is the sub-district of Aldeburgh, and Friston is shown as the first place within it. The list shows that the piece reference for the returns for this area is RG 10/1765. This is then used to order the appropriate reel of microfilm.

Many local record offices and libraries have used the PRO reference system explained above to produce their own indexes to the returns they have on microfilm. Some repositories, however, have indexed their holdings according to the references they have given to the reels of census microfilm purchased from the PRO. Rather than giving the full PRO reference, a place is said to be on 'Reel 1' or some other reference meaningful to the repository. This system of numbering should be avoided at all costs since such references do not uniquely identify each frame of the microfilm, and it is unlikely that any replacement microfilm purchased in due course will contain exactly the same pieces and folios.

For very small places which are not mentioned in the placename indexes it may be necessary to use topographical gazetteers to discover within which larger administrative area they fell. This may be especially necessary when they were ecclesiastical areas overlapping civil administrative boundaries. Care should be taken to ensure that the gazetteer used is as near as possible contemporary to the relevant census since boundary changes may affect administrative areas.

In those cases where places cannot be found in gazetteers, recourse can be had to contemporary maps, especially those produced by the Ordnance Survey. Local repositories will usually have a collection of maps of the area. A particularly useful set of such documents can be found in the PRO record class RG 18.[4] This is a series of maps showing the boundaries of the registration districts and sub-districts for various dates in the late nineteenth, and early twentieth, centuries. The originals are kept at the PRO Kew but a microfilm version is kept at Portugal Street. The originals are not particularly robust and excessive use by readers would damage them irreparably.

In the case of many large towns the PRO and other repositories hold street indexes. The PRO only has such indexes for places with a population over 40,000 but some local repositories have such finding aids for smaller places which appear in the microfilm copies they hold. Not every large town has an index for every census year.

Street indexes can be very complicated and a description of their workings is best left until one actually consults them at the archive. They are often arranged by registration district, sub-district, and enumeration district numbers, rather than by PRO piece, folio and page references, and it is necessary to use tables to convert the former into the latter. Streets

---

4   Reference Maps of Registrars' Districts (PRO: RG 18).

might run through several enumeration districts, and one may have to look through several different pieces to find the right address. One should remember, however, the problems associated with addresses outlined in Chapter 8. In all cases those preparing such indexes should use the PRO reference system outlined above, since this is the only way of ensuring that indexes are compatible.

Many local family history societies have produced surname indexes for particular areas, mostly for the 1851 census. The PRO has a collection of some of these but recourse may more profitably be had to the local societies themselves. The addresses of local societies can be obtained through the Federation of Family History Societies.[5] The Society of Genealogists[6] attempts to acquire all census transcripts and indexes as they become available. The PRO, of course, welcomes the donation of any indexes of this type.

Some locally produced surname indexes are defective in certain respects. Some fail to give PRO references, giving idiosyncratic references of their own, or quoting the reel numbers in local repositories. This makes it impossible to use these indexes in the PRO, or other local record offices and libraries. Some only refer to the names of heads of households, or to surnames without christian names. It becomes extremely tedious to go through a large number of entries for families called 'Smith', before coming across the household required. Complete indexes to all persons in an area, giving christian names as well as surnames, are always to be preferred.

The census on computer

For those historians who have access to a mainframe computer, and are interested in national or regional studies, it may be unnecessary for them to collect their own sample data from the census. A two per cent clustered sample of the 1851 returns for England, Wales, and Scotland, has been deposited in machine-readable form at the ESRC Data Archive.[7] This sample, the work of a team at the University of Edinburgh under Professor Michael Anderson, is available whole or in sub-sets. Details of the database, and the scale of charges for access, are available from the archive.

It should be noted, however, that, because of the changes to the definition of the household outlined in Chapter 9, the results of any analysis of household structure based on this data may not be strictly comparable with populations in other censuses.

Missing returns

Regretably the surviving census returns are not a full record of the population of nineteenth-century England and Wales, and it may thus be impossible to track down an individual or community. These omissions, which are fortunately not too extensive, reflect both under-enumeration at the time of the census, and subsequent loss or damage to the returns.

---

5   c/o Mrs Pauline Saul, 31 Seven Star Road, Solihull, W Midlands, B91 2B2.
6   14 Charterhouse Buildings, Goswell Road, London, EC1M 7BA.
7   ESRC Data Archive, University of Essex, Wivenhoe Park, Colchester, Essex, CO4 3SQ.

In the early censuses under the GRO certain groups, usually those not living in conventional households, were simply not enumerated by name. These included the members of the Royal Navy on board ship in 1841, and possibly 1851; all members of the merchant marine in 1841, and various sections of it thereafter; all fishermen afloat in 1841, and sections of this group thereafter; the crews of vessels engaged in inland navigation in 1841 and 1851; and all itinerants, travellers and nightworkers in 1841, and probably a considerable number of the same in later years. The soldiers serving abroad were never enumerated by name. All these groups have been considered in more detail in Chapter 7.

Enumerators and householders inevitably made slips in recording or copying. A house may be omitted, perhaps because it was unoccupied on census night, and the enumerator forgot to note it down as empty; a wife may be absent because of an enumerator's copying blunder; a new-born child may be temporarily lost sight of; and so on. Wrigley and Schofield have calculated, for example, that the censuses of 1841 to 1871 record approximately five per cent fewer children aged under five than would be expected from vital registration data.[8]

Undoubtedly some households will have completely slipped through the census net. There is no way of telling how many, of course, because we have no other source to compare the census with. It should be noted, however, that post-enumeration surveys for the 1981 census indicated that 0.5% of households were missed in that census in the whole of England and Wales. In Inner London in 1981, however, the under-enumeration may have been of the order of 2.75%.[9] Similar or greater levels of omission might be expected in nineteenth-century censuses.

Lastly, some of the original returns, which were not kept in optimum archival conditions in the nineteenth century, have been lost or damaged. Often such damage was confined to the backs and fronts of enumeration books but more extensive gaps exist. Special returns, such as those for shipping, which were often appended to the back of enumerators' books were especially liable to damage. In 1841 the Kensington, Paddington, Golden Lane and Whitecross sub-districts of London are missing from the returns, as are parts of Kent and Essex. In Denbighshire at the same date the books covering the hundred of Bromfield are missing, as are parts of the hundreds of Yale, Rhuthun and Isaled. In 1851 the returns for Salford and parts of Manchester have been severely damaged by water. The ships' returns for this census also seem to have been destroyed at some stage. In 1861 the Belgravia and Woolwich Arsenal sub-districts (containing 75,000 people) are missing. The list of such problems could be greatly extended but this would soon become tedious. The only comprehensive guide to such gaps is to be found in the class lists at the PRO.

---

8   E A Wrigley and R S Schofield, *The population history of England 1541–1871* (London, 1981), pp 589–590.
9   F Whitehead, 'The GRO use of social surveys', p 46.

Appendix 1   Census Acts and Census Days, England and Wales, 1801–1901

Census		Census Act
Year	Day	Reference and date
1801	Monday, 10 March	41 Geo. III c. 15 31 December 1800
1811	Monday, 27 May	51 Geo. III c. 6 22 March 1811
1821	Monday, 28 May	1 Geo. IV c. 94 24 July 1820
1831	Monday, 30 May	11 Geo. IV & 1 Will. IV c. 30 23 June 1830
1841	Sunday, 6 June	3 & 4 Vict. c. 99 10 August 1840
		4 & 5 Vict. c. 7 6 April 1841
1851	Sunday, 30 March	13 & 14 Vict. c. 53 5 August 1850
1861	Sunday, 7 April	23 & 24 Vict. c. 61 6 August 1860
1871	Sunday, 2 April	33 & 34 Vict. c. 107 10 August 1870
1881	Sunday, 3 April	43 & 44 Vict. c. 37 7 September 1880
1891	Sunday, 5 April	53 & 54 Vict. c. 61 18 August 1890
1901	Sunday, 31 March	63 & 64 Vict. c. 4 27 March 1900

Appendix 2 The overall structure of the enumeration books

1841

Unnumbered pages at beginning of book:

Page i	Geographical information – both ancient divisions (county, hundred, parish, etc.) and those for registration purposes (superintendent registrar's district, registrar's district, number of enumeration district). Description of enumeration district.
Page ii	Blank.
Page iii	Extract from Census Act regarding the penalty for refusing information or giving false answers.
Page iv	Directions for filling up the book.
Page v	Example of how to fill up the book.
Pages $1 - x$	Pages for the insertion of nominal information numbered one to x.

The last three pages continue the numbering of the above, which was therefore dependent on the number of such pages in the book:

First page	Summary table of the total number of houses and persons in each of the foregoing pages.
Second page	Summary tables regarding itinerants, the temporary increase and decrease of the population, and emigration.
Third page	Declarations signed by the enumerator, registrar and superintendent registrar.

Overall dimensions: 13" high by 8¼" wide.

1851

Page i	Description of enumeration district with geographical data.
Page ii	Summary table of the total number of houses, occupiers, and persons in each of the pages for nominal information.

| Page iii | Summary tables for the number of itinerants and the temporary increase and decrease of the population. |

Page iii   Summary tables for the number of itinerants and the temporary increase and decrease of the population.

Page iv   Declarations signed by the enumerator, registrar and superintendent registrar.

Page v   Directions for filling up the book.

Pages vi – vii   Example of how to fill up the book.

Pages 1 – x   Pages for inserting nominal information.

Overall dimensions: 8″ high by 12½″ wide.

1861

Page i   Description of enumeration district with geographical data.

Page ii   Directions for filling up the book.

Page iii   Example of how to fill up the book.

Page iv   Summary tables for the number of itinerants and the temporary increase and decrease of the population.

Page v   Summary table of the total number of houses, persons and schedules in each of the pages for nominal information.

Page vi   Declarations signed by the enumerator, registrar and superintendent registrar.

Pages 1 – x   Pages for inserting nominal information.

Overall dimensions: 9¼″ high by 14½″ wide.

1871

Page i   Description of enumeration district with geographical data.

Page ii   Directions for filling up the book.

Page iii   Example of how to fill up the book.

Page iv   Summary tables for the temporary increase and decrease of the population, and the number of houses, persons and schedules by geographical division.

Page v   Summary table of the total number of houses, persons and schedules in each of the pages for nominal information.

Page vi   Declarations signed by the enumerator, registrar and superintendent registrar.

Pages 1 – x   Pages for inserting nominal information.

Overall dimensions: 9¼″ high by 14½″ wide.

1881

Page i	Description of enumeration district with geographical data.
Page ii	Directions for filling up the book.
Page iii	Example of how to fill up the book.
Page iv	Summary tables for the temporary increase and decrease of the population, and the number of houses, persons and schedules by geographical division.
Page v	Summary table of the total number of houses, persons and schedules in each of the pages for nominal information.
Page vi	Declarations signed by the enumerator, registrar and superintendent registrar.
Pages 1 – x	Pages for inserting nominal information.

Overall dimensions: 9¼″ high by 14½″ wide.

1891

Page i	Description of enumeration district with geographical data.
Page ii	Directions for filling up the book.
Page iii	Example of how to fill up the book.
Page iv	Summary tables for the number of houses, persons and schedules by geographical division.
Page v	Summary table of the total number of houses, persons and schedules and tenements of less than five rooms in each of the pages for nominal information.
Page vi	Declarations signed by the enumerator, registrar and superintendent registrar.
Pages 1 – x	Pages for inserting nominal information.

Overall dimensions: 11¼″ high by 17″ wide.

1901

These returns are closed to public inspection but are likely to be similar to those for 1891.

Appendix 3   The structure of the nominal page

Column	Heading	Subheading		Comments
1841				
1	Place			i.e. address
2	Houses	1	uninhabited or being built	
		2	inhabited	
3	Names			
4	Age and Sex	1	males	
		2	females	
5	Profession, trade, employment or of independent means			
6	Where born	1	whether born in same county	'Y' or 'N' for yes or no
		2	whether born in Scotland, Ireland or foreign parts	'S', 'I', or 'F' for Scotland, Ireland, or foreign parts
1851				
1	Number of schedule			numbered from 1 consecutively
2	Name of street, place or road, and name or number of house			
3	Name and surname			
4	Relation to head of family			
5	Condition			i.e. marital status
6	Age	1	males	
		2	females	

Column	Heading	Subheading		Comments
	Heading	*Subheading*		*Comments*
7	Rank, profession or occupation			
8	Where born			county: place
9	Whether blind or deaf-and-dumb			

1861

1	Number of schedule			numbered from 1 consecutively
2	Road, street, etc., and number or name of house			
3	Houses	1	inhabited	
		2	uninhabited	'U' for uninhabited: 'B' for being built
4	Name and surname			
5	Relation to head of family			
6	Condition			i.e. marital status
7	Age	1	males	
		2	females	
8	Rank, profession or occupation			
9	Where born			county: place
10	Whether blind or deaf-and-dumb			

1871

1	Number of schedule			numbered from 1 consecutively
2	Road, street, etc., and number or name of house			
3	Houses	1	inhabited	
		2	uninhabited	'U' for uninhabited: 'B' for being built
4	Name and surname			

Column	Heading	Subheading	Comments
5	Relation to head of family		
6	Condition		i.e. marital status
7	Age	1 males 2 females	
8	Rank, profession or occupation		
9	Where born		county: place
10	Whether 1 Deaf-and-dumb 2 Blind 3 Imbecile or idiot 4 Lunatic		

1881

Column	Heading	Subheading	Comments
1	Number of schedule		numbered from 1 consecutively
2	Road, street, etc., and number or name of house		
3	Houses	1 inhabited 2 uninhabited	'U' for uninhabited: 'B' for being built
4	Name and surname		
5	Relation to head of family		
6	Condition as to marriage		i.e. marital status
7	Age last birthday	1 males 2 females	
8	Rank, profession or occupation		
9	Where born		county: place
10	Whether 1 Deaf-and-dumb 2 Blind 3 Imbecile or idiot 4 Lunatic		

Column	Heading	Subheading		Comments

1891

1	Number of schedule			numbered from 1 consecutively
2	Road, street, etc., number or name of house			
3	Houses	1	inhabited	
		2	uninhabited	'U' for uninhabited: 'B' for being built
4	Number of rooms occupied if less than five			
5	Name and surname			
6	Relation to head of family			
7	Condition as to marriage			i.e. marital status
8	Age last birthday	1	males	
		2	females	
9	Profession or occupation			
10	Employer			insert 'X'
11	Employed			insert 'X'
12	Neither employer nor employed			insert 'X'
13	Where born			county: place
14	Whether			
	1 Deaf-and-dumb			
	2 Blind			
	3 Lunatic, imbecile, or idiot			

Column	Heading	Subheading		Comments

1901

1	Number of schedule			numbered from 1 consecutively
2	Road, street, etc., number or name of house			
3	Houses	1	inhabited	insert '1'
		2	in occupation	insert '1'
		3	not in occupation	insert '1'
		4	being built	insert '1'
4	Number of rooms occupied if less than five			
5	Name and surname			
6	Relation to head of family			
7	Condition as to marriage			i.e. marital status
8	Age last birthday	1	males	
		2	females	
9	Profession or occupation			
10	Employer, worker, or own account			answer to be written
11	If working at home			answer to be written
12	Where born			county: place
13	Whether			
	1 Deaf-and-dumb			
	2 Blind			
	3 Lunatic			
	4 Imbecile, feeble-minded			

41° GEORGII III. Cap. 15.

FORM of ANSWERS by the OVERSEERS, &c. in ENGLAND,

To the Questions contained in the Schedule to an Act, intituled, *An Act for taking an Account of the Population of Great Britain, and of the Increase or Diminution thereof.*

County, &c.	Hundred, &c.	City, Town, &c.	Parish, &c.	QUESTION 1st. HOUSES.			QUESTION 2d. PERSONS, including Children of whatever Age.			QUESTION 3d. OCCUPATIONS.			TOTAL of PERSONS.
				Inhabited.	By how many Families occupied.	Uninhabited.	Males.	Females.	Total of PERSONS in Answer to Question 2d.	Persons chiefly employed in Agriculture.	Persons chiefly employed in Trade, Manufactures, or Handicraft.	All other Persons not comprised in the Two preceding Classes.	N. B. This Column must correspond with the Total of Persons in Answer to Question 2d.

N. B. If any Family occupies Two or more Houses in different Parishes, Townships, or Places, the Individuals belonging to such Family are to be numbered only in those Parishes, Townships, or Places where they severally happen to be at the Time of taking the Account.

REMARKS, in Explanation of the Matters stated in Answer to the preceding Questions.

1st Question.
2d Question.
3d Question.

ATTESTATION on Oath (or Affirmation) by the OVERSEERS or substantial Householders in ENGLAND.

I, *A. B.* One of the Overseers (or a substantial Householder) of the Parish, Township, &c. of   in the County of   do swear (or affirm), That the above Return contains, to the best of my Knowledge and Belief, a full and true Answer to the Questions contained in the Schedule to an Act, intituled, *An Act for taking an Account of the Population of Great Britain, and of the Increase or Diminution thereof.*

The above-mentioned *A. B.* was sworn (or affirmed) before us the Justices of the Peace in and for the   of   this   Day of

C. D. and *E. F.*

1801 enumeration schedule

58   51° GEORGII III.   Cap. 6.

FORM of Answers by the OVERSEERS, &c. in England, and Schoolmasters, &c. in Scotland, to the Questions contained in the Schedule to an Act, 51 Geo. III. intituled, " An Act for taking an Account of the Population of Great Britain, and of the Increase or Diminution thereof."

Name and Description of Parish, &c.	Question 1st.		Question 2d.	Question 3d.	Question 4th. OCCUPATIONS.		Question 5th. Persons, including Children, of whatever Age.		
	Inhabited Houses.	By how many Families occupied.	Houses now building.	Other Houses uninhabited.	Families chiefly employed in Agriculture.	Families chiefly employed in Trade, Manufactures, and Handicraft.	All other Families not comprized in the Two preceding Classes.	Males.	Females.	Total of Persons.

N. B. If any Family occupies Two or more Houses in different Parishes, Townships, or Places, the Individuals belonging to such Family are to be numbered only in those Parishes, Townships, or Places, where they severally happen to be at the Time of taking the Account.

6th Question.   Referring to the Number of Persons in 1801, To what Cause do you attribute any remarkable Difference in the Number at present ?

7th Question.   Are there any other Matters, which you may think it necessary to remark, in Explanation of your Answers to any of the preceding Questions ?

ATTESTATION on Oath [or, Affirmation] by the Overseers or substantial Householders in England, and by the Schoolmasters in Scotland.

I, A. B. One of the Overseers, Schoolmaster [or, a substantial Householder] of the Parish, Township, &c. of   in the County of   Do [wear [or, affirm] That the above Return contains, to the best of my Knowledge and Belief, a full and true Answer to the Questions contained in the Schedule to an Act, intituled, " An Act for taking an Account of the Population of Great Britain, and of the Increase or Diminution thereof."

The above-mentioned A. B. was sworn [or, affirmed] (in England) before us the Justices of the Peace in and for the   of   C. D. and E. F.
this   Day of

this   Day of   (in Scotland) before me the Sheriff Depute of the   of   •   G. H.

1811 enumeration schedule

1° GEORGII IV. Cap. 94. 771

FORM of Answer by the OVERSEERS, &c. in England, and Schoolmasters, &c. in Scotland, to the Questions contained in the Schedule to an Act, 1st Geo. IV., intituled " An Act for taking an Account of the Population of Great Britain, and of the Increase or Diminution thereof."

Name and Description of Parish, &c., and within what County, Hundred, Town Corporate, or other Division situate.	Question 1st.		Question 2d.	Question 3d.	Question 4th. OCCUPATIONS.			Question 5th. Persons, including Children, of whatever Age.		
	Inhabited Houses.	By how many Families occupied.	Houses now building.	Other Houses uninhabited.	Families chiefly employed in Agriculture.	Families chiefly employed in Trade, Manufactures, and Handicraft.	All other Families not comprised in the Two preceding Classes.	Males.	Females.	Total of Persons.

N.B. If any Family occupies Two or more Houses in different Parishes, Townships, or Places, the Individuals belonging to such Family are to be numbered only in those Parishes, Townships, or Places, where they severally happen to be at the Time of taking the Account.

6th Question. Referring to the Number of Persons in 1811, To what Cause do you attribute any remarkable Difference in the Number at present?

7th Question. Are there any other Matters, which you may think it necessary to remark, in Explanation of your Answers to any of the preceding Questions?

ATTESTATION on Oath [or, Affirmation] by the Overseers or substantial Householders in England, and by the Schoolmasters in Scotland.

I, A.B. One of the Overseers, Schoolmaster [or, a substantial Householder] of the Parish, Township, &c. of _____ in the County of _____ do swear [or, affirm] That the above Return contains, to the best of my Knowledge and Belief, a full and true Answer to the Questions contained in the Schedule to an Act, intituled " An Act for taking an Account of the Population of Great Britain, and of the Increase or Diminution thereof."

The above-mentioned A.B. was sworn [or, affirmed] (in England) before us the Justices of the Peace in and for the _____ of _____ C.D. and E.F.
this _____ Day of _____

(in Scotland) before me the Sheriff Depute or Substitute of the _____ of _____ G.H.
this _____ Day of _____

1821 enumeration schedule

314   **11° GEORGII   IV.   Cap.30.**

FORM of ANSWER by the OVERSEERS, &c. in England, and SCHOOLMASTERS, &c. in Scotland, to the Questions contained in the Schedule to an Act, 11th George 4th, intituled "An Act for taking an Account of the Population of Great Britain, and of the Increase or Diminution thereof."

Name and Description of Parish, &c. and within what County, Hundred, Town Corporate, or other Division situate.	QUESTION 1st.		QUESTION 2d.	QUESTION 3d.	QUESTION 4th. OCCUPATIONS.			QUESTION 5th. Persons, including Children, of whatever Age.		
	Inhabited Houses.	By how many Families occupied.	Houses now building.	Other Houses uninhabited.	Families chiefly employed in Agriculture.	Families chiefly employed in Trade, Manufactures, and Handicraft.	All other Families not comprised in the Two preceding Classes.	Males.	Females.	Total of Persons.

N. B. — Individuals are to be numbered only in those Parishes, Townships, or Places where they severally happen to be at the Time of taking the Account.

QUESTION 6th.	QUESTION 7th. Males employed in Agriculture.			QUESTION 8th.	QUESTION 9th.	QUESTION 10th.	QUESTION 11th.	QUESTION 12th.
Total Number of Males Twenty Years old.	Occupiers of Land employing Labourers.	Occupiers of Land not employing Labourers.	Labourers employed in Agriculture.	Males employed in Manufacture, or in making Manufacturing Machinery.	Males employed in Retail Trade, or in Handicraft, as Masters or Workmen.	Wholesale Merchants, Capitalists, Bankers, Professional Persons, and other Educated Men.	Labourers employed by the Three preceding Classes, and in other Labour not Agricultural.	All other Males Twenty Years old (except Servants), including retired Tradesmen, superannuated Labourers, and Males diseased or disabled in Body or Mind.

1831 enumeration schedule, Part 1

11° GEORGII IV. Cap. 30.   315

QUESTION 13th. — HOW many Servants, distinguishing Males upwards of Twenty Years old ——, Males under Twenty Years old ——, Females —— ?

QUESTION 14th. — IF you have entered any Males in answer to the 8th Question, be pleased to specify the Manufacture or Manufactures in which they are employed? And what Proportion of the Number of those entered in answer to Question 11th, are employed in any Quarry, Mines, Coal Pits, Fishery, or Public Work now in progress?

QUESTION 15th. — REFERRING to the Number of Persons in 1821, to what Cause do you attribute any remarkable Difference in the Number at present?

QUESTION 16th. — ARE there any other Matters which you may think it necessary to remark, in explanation of your Answers to any of the preceding Questions?

ATTESTATION on Oath [or Affirmation] by the Overseers or substantial Householders in England, and by the Schoolmasters in Scotland.

I, A. B. One of the Overseers, Schoolmaster, [or a substantial Householder] of the Parish, Township, &c. of —— in the County of —— do swear [or affirm], That the above Return contains, to the best of my Knowledge and Belief, a full and true Answer to the Questions contained in the Schedule to an Act, intituled "An Act for taking an Account of the Population of Great Britain, and of the Increase or Diminution thereof."

The above-mentioned A. B. was sworn [or affirmed] (in England) before us, the Justices of the Peace in and for the C. D. and E. F. Day of —— this —— of ——

(In Scotland) The above-mentioned A. B. was sworn before me, the Sheriff Depute or Substitute of the —— of —— this —— Day of —— G. H.

The above Answers, collected and arranged by A. B., are [or are not] (in my Opinion) correct.   I. K. Minister of the Parish of ——

1831 enumeration schedule, Part 2

11° GEORGII IV. Cap. 30.   317

ANSWER TO THIRD QUESTION.

PARISH of   REGISTERED BURIALS, 1813.

Column 1.			Column 2.			Column 3.			Column 4.		
Ages.	Males.	Females.	Ages.	Males.	Females.	Ages.	Males.	Females.	Ages.	Males.	Females.
Under One Year.			3			26			58		
						27			59		
						28			60		
			4			29			61		
						30			62		
						31			63		
						32			64		
						33			65		
			5			34			66		
						35			67		
						36			68		
						37			69		
			6			38			70		
			7			39			71		
			8			40			72		
			9			41			73		
			10			42			74		
			11			43			75		
			12			44			76		
			13			45			77		
			14			46			78		
			15			47			79		
1			16			48			80		
			17			49			81		
			18			50			82		
			19			51			83		
			20			52			84		
			21			53					
			22			54					
2			23			55					
			24			56					
			25			57					

		SUMMARY.		
			Males.	Females.	Total.

Defective Registry of Ages   -

In Burial Grounds of Dissenters, Jews, and others

1st Column   -   -
2nd Column   -   -
3rd Column   -   -
4th Column   -   -

[*Eighteen similar Pages, numbered consecutively 1813–1850, are to be transmitted to every officiating Minister in England.*]

4 L

1831 Page from the clergyman's return of the ages of persons being buried, 1813–1830

City or Borough of *Southwark*   **36**

Parish or Township of *St Saviour*   { *Example of Enumeration Schedule,* }
{ *shewing how Entries may be made.* }

PLACE.	HOUSES		NAMES of each Person who abode therein the preceding Night.	AGE and SEX.		PROFESSION, TRADE, EMPLOYMENT, or of INDEPENDENT MEANS.	Where Born	
	Uninhabited or Building.	Inhabited.		Males.	Females.		Whether Born in same County.	Whether Born in Scotland, Ireland, or Foreign Parts.
George Street		1	James Johnson	40		Chemist	Y.	
			Jane do.		35		N.	
			William do.	15		Shoem. Ap.	Y.	
			Anne do.		13		Y.	
			Edward Smith	20		Chemist's Sh.	N.	
			Sarah Robins		45	F. S.		I.
do.	126	1	John Cox	60		Publican	N.	
do.	1 B		Mary do.		45		Y.	
do.	1 B		Ellen do.		20		N.	
			James Macpherson	25		M. S.		S.
			Henry Wilson	35		Army	N.	
			n. k.	above 20				
Extra Parochial Place, named The Close.		1	William Jones	50		Farmer	Y.	
			Elizabeth do.		40		Y.	
			William do.	15		Navy	Y.	
			Charlotte do.		8		Y.	
			n. k. do.		5 months		Y.	
			Richard Clerk	20		Ag. Lab.	N.	
do.	126	1	Robert Hall	45		Tailor	Y.	
			Martha do.		30		Y.	
			John Multer	25		Tailor J.		F.
			Ann Williams		20	F. S.	N.	
Chapel Row.		1	Edward Jackson	35		Ind.	N.	
			Charles do.	30		Cl.	N.	
			James Leary	20		M. S.		I.
TOTAL in Page	2bb 2 B	5		15	10			

B b

1841 enumerator's return

vi

[Example of the manner in which Entries should be made in the Schedule Book.]

Parish or Township of St. James, Westminster   Ecclesiastical District of   City or Borough of Westminster   Town of

No. of Householder's Schedule	Name of Street, Place, or Road, and Name or No. of House	Name and Surname of each Person who abode in the house, on the Night of the 30th March, 1851	Relation to Head of Family	Condition	Age of Males	Females	Rank, Profession, or Occupation	Where Born	Whether Blind, or Deaf-and-Dumb
4	7. Charlotte Street	Michael Mangen	Head	Mar.	20		Victualler	Ireland.	
		Mary Do.	Wife	Mar.		30		Ireland.	
		Ellen Do.	Daur.			7m.		Middlesex; St. Jas. Westmr.	
		Catherine Fox	Serv.	Do.		30	General Serv.	Hants; Andover.	
		Catherine Doyle	Serv.	Do.		25	Housemaid	Ireland.	
5	8 Charlotte Street	Lambert Locken	Head	Mar.	30		Tea-dealer; (master, employing one man)	Cumberland; Wigton.	
		Emma Do.	Wife	Mar.		30		Cumberland; Longtown.	
		William Do.	Son		2			Middlesex; St. Jas. Westmr.	Deaf & Dumb
		Henrietta Do.	Daur.			4m.		Do. ; Do.	
		George Betts	Shopman	Do.	19		Tea-dealer's Shopman	Do. ; Shoreditch.	
		Jane Cook	Serv.	Do.		22	General Serv.	Do. ; Mary-le-bone.	
6		James Phillips	Head	Mar.	40		Plumber	Yorkshire; Leeds.	
		Harriet Do.	Wife	Mar.		30		Do. ; Do.	
		Sophia White	Serv.	Mar.		13	General Serv.	Middlesex; St. Jas. Westmr.	
	Three Houses uninhabited								
7	2 Bird Lane	William Frampton	Head	Do.	72		Coach Trimmer	Stafford; Bidston.	
		Anne Do.	Wife	Mar.		74		Do. Do.	
8	3 Bird Lane	Thomas Johnson	Head	Widr.	68		Retired Grocer	Devonshire; Honiton.	
		Emma Do.	Niece	Do.		41	Corset Maker	Middlesex; St. Pancras.	
		Jane Farmer	Apprentice	Do.		15	Corset Maker (appr.)	Middlesex; Popney.	
Total of Houses: I 4; U 3; B —				Total of Males and Females ...	7	13			

1851 enumerator's return

iii

80

[Example]

The undermentioned Houses are situate within the Boundaries of the

Ecclesiastical District of Christchurch

No. of Schedule	Road, Street, &c., and No. or Name of House	Houses Inhabited	Houses Uninhabited (U.B.)	Name and Surname of each Person	Relation to Head of Family	Condition	Age Males	Age Females	Rank, Profession, or Occupation	Where Born	Whether Blind, or Deaf-and-Dumb
4	7, Charlotte St "Queen's Arms"	1		Michael Monson	Head	Mar.	31		Victualler	Middlesex; Islington	
				Mary A. Do.	Wife	Mar.		29		Salop; Condover	
				Ellen Do.	Dau.			7mo		Surrey; St Saviour, Southwark	
				Ann Fox	Serv.	Un.		28	General Serv.	Hants; Andover	
				Madeline Doyle	Serv.	Un.		24	Barmaid	Ireland	
5	8, Charlotte St	1		Lambert Newton	Head	Mar.	39		Grocer; (master, employing 2 men)	Cumberland; Wigton	
				Emma Do.	Wife	Mar.		36		Cumberland; Longtown	
				William Do.	Son		12		Scholar	Surrey; St Saviour, Southwark	
				Henrietta Do.	Dau.			9	Do.	Do.	
6				George Bacon	Shopman	Un.	19		Grocer's Shopman	Middlesex; Shoreditch	
				Jane Cook	Serv.	Un.		22	General Serv.	Marylebone	
				James F. Phillips	Serv.	Mar.	44		Bricklayer's Cl.	Yorkshire; Leeds	
				Laura Do.	Wife	Mar.		29		Do.; Bradford	
				Sophia White	Serv.	Un.		16	General Serv.	Middlesex; St Sav., Westminster	
7	9, 10, 11, Do — 1, Bird Lane		3 W.	William Hampton	Head	Mar.	72		Coach Trimmer	Staffords; Bilston	
				Anne Do.	Wife	Mar.		69		Do.; Tamworth	
8	2, Bird Lane	1		Thomas Johnson	Head	Widr	68		Retired Grocer	Devon; London	
				Emma Do.	Niece	Un.		44	Cowel Maker	Middlesex; St Pancras	
				Jane Eames	Apprentice	Un.		18	Cowel Maker (App)	Middlesex; Stepney	
				Walter Johnson	Lodger	Un.	23		Ship Carpenter	Durham; Sunderland	
9	Do.		2 B.								

End of Christchurch Ecclesiastical District

Total of Houses... 4	3 U. 2 B.	Total of Males and Females...	8	12

City or Municipal Borough of Southwark — Municipal Ward of High Street — Parliamentary Borough of Southwark — Township of St Saviour

57

iii.

[Example]

The undermentioned Houses are situate within the Boundaries of the

Civil Parish [or Township] of St. Mary.	City or Municipal Borough of Shrewsbury.	Municipal Ward of High Street.	Parliamentary Borough of Shrewsbury.	Town [not being a City or Borough] of	Village or Hamlet, &c. of	Local Board [or Improvement Commissioners District] of Shrewsbury.	Ecclesiastical District of St. Michael.

| No. of Schedule | Road, Street, &c. and No. or Name of House | HOUSES | | Name and Surname of each Person | Relation to Head of Family | Condition | Age of | | Rank, Profession, or Occupation | Where Born | Whether 1. Deaf-and-Dumb 2. Blind 3. Imbecile or Idiot 4. Lunatic |
		In-habited	Un-inhabited (U.) or Building (B.)				Males	Female			
4	2, Charlotte St. ["Queen's Arms"]	1		Michael Mattison	Head	Mar.	31		Licensed Victualler	Middlesex; Islington.	
				Mary J. Do.	Wife	Mar.		29		Salop; Cardover.	
				Ellen Do.	Daur.			7 mo.		Salop; Shrewsbury.	
				Elizabeth Mattison	Mother	W.		58	Annuitant	Salop; Shrewsbury.	Lunatic.
				Ann Fox	Serv.	Unm.		28	General Serv.	Scords; Andover.	
				Catherine Doyle	Serv.	Unm.		24	Barmaid	Ireland.	
5	8, Charlotte St.	1		Lambert Newton	Head	Mar.	39		Grocer; (master, employing 2 men)	Cumberland; Weston.	
				Emma Do.	Wife	Mar.		36		Do.; Longtown.	
				William Do.	Son		9		Scholar	Salop; Pullтом.	
				Henrietta Do.	Daur.			12	Do.	Do.; Do.	
				George Bacon	Shopman	Unm.	19		Grocer's Shopman	Middlesex; Shoreditch.	
				Jane Cock	Serv.	Unm.		22	General Serv.	Scotland.	
6		1		James L. Phillips	Head	Mar.	44		Banker's Clerk	Yorkshire; Leeds.	
				Harriet Do.	Wife	Mar.		39		Do.; Bradford.	D. & Dumb from Birth.
				Sophia White	Serv.	Unm.		16	General Serv.	Salop; Bridgenorth.	

7	6, Do.	1		William Thompson	Head	Mar.	72		Coach Trimmer	Staffordsh.; Bilston.	
	4, Bird Lane			Jane Do.	Wife	Mar.		69		Do.; Tamworth.	
8	2, Bird Lane	1		Thomas Johnson	Head	Wid.	68		Retired Grocer	Devon; Honiton.	
				Henry Johnson	Son	Unm.	39		Organist	Salop; Shrewsbury.	Blind from Seatt Pox.
				Emma Do.	Niece	Unm.		41	Gonvt Males	Middlesex; St. Pancras.	
				Jane Turner	Apprentice	Unm.	18		Court Males (Apprentice)	Salop; Pullтом.	
1	Do.	2 U. 2 B.		Walter Campbell	Lodger	Unm.	23		Ship Carpenter (out of employ)	Durham; Sunderland.	

| | | | | End of St. Michael Ecclesiastical District | | | | | | | |

| Total of Houses... | 4 | 1 U. 2 B. | | | | Total of Males and Females... | 9 | 13 | | | |

1871 enumerator's return

iii.

The undermentioned Houses are situate within the Boundaries of the

Civil Parish [or Township] of St. Mary.	City or Municipal Borough of Shrewsbury.	Municipal Ward of Welsh.	Parliamentary Borough of Shrewsbury.	Town or Village or Hamlet of —	Urban Sanitary District of Shrewsbury.	Rural Sanitary District of —	Ecclesiastical Parish or District of St. Michael. 51

[Example]

No. of Schedule	ROAD, STREET, &c., and No. or NAME of HOUSE	HOUSES Inhabited	HOUSES Uninhabited (U.), or building (B.)	NAME and Surname of each Person	RELATION to Head of Family	CONDITION as to Marriage	AGE last Birthday of Males	AGE last Birthday of Females	Rank, Profession, or OCCUPATION	WHERE BORN	If (1)Deaf-&-Dumb (2)Blind (3)Imbecile or Idiot (4)Lunatic
4	7, Charlotte St. ["Queen's Arms"]	1		Michael Morrison	Head	Mar.	31		Licensed Victualler	Middlesex; Islington	
				Mary J. Do.	Wife	Mar.		29		Salop; Condover	
				Ellen Do.	Daur.			7mo.		Salop; Shrewsbury	
				Elizabeth Morrison	Mother	W.		58	Annuitant	Salop; Shrewsbury	Lunatic
				Ann Fox	Serv.	Unm.		28	General Serv.	Hants; Andover	
				Catherine Doyle	Serv.	Unm.		24	Barmaid	Ireland	
5	8, Charlotte St.	1		Lambert Newton	Head	Mar.	39		Grocer; (master, employing 2 men)	Cumberland; Weston	
				Emma Do.	Wife	Mar.		36		Do.; Longtown	
				William Do.	Son		12		Scholar	Salop; Ludlow	
				Henrietta Do.	Daur.			8	Do.	Do.; Do.	Deaf-and-Dumb
				George Bacon	Shopman	Unm.	19		Grocer's Shopman	Middlesex; Shoreditch	
				Jane Cook	Serv.	Unm.		22	General Serv.	Scotland	
6				James P. Phillips	Head	Mar.	41		Banker's Clerk	Yorkshire; Leeds	
				Harriet Do.	Wife	Mar.		41		Do.; Blandford	
				Sophia White	Serv.	Unm.		16	General Serv.	Salop; Bridgnorth	
7	1, Bird Lane	1		William Hampton	Head	Mar.	72		Coach Trimmer	Staffordsh.; Bilston	
	Do.			Anne Do.	Wife	Mar.		69		Do.; Tamworth	
8	2, Bird Lane	1		Thomas Johnson	Head	Wid.	68		Retired Grocer	Devon; Honiton	
				Henry Johnson	Son	Unm.	32		Organist	Salop; Shrewsbury	
				Emma Do.	Niece	Unm.		44		Middlesex; St. Pancras	
				Jane James	Apprentice	Unm.		18	Corset Maker (Apprentice)	Salop; Ludlow	Blind
9	Do.	2 B.		Walter Campbell	Lodger	Unm.	23		Ship Carpenter (out of employ)	Durham; Sunderland	
						Out of St. Michael Ecclesiastical District					
	Total of Houses... 4	4	1 U. 2 B.	Total of Males and Females...	End of	St. Michael Ecclesiastical District	9	13			

1881 enumerator's return

[EXAMPLE]

57

Administrative County of R. Anne.

Civil Parish of R. Anne	Municipal Borough of Shrewsbury	Municipal Ward of Welsh	Urban Sanitary District of Shrewsbury	Town & Village & Hamlet of	Rural Sanitary District of	Parliamentary Borough or Division of Shrewsbury	Ecclesiastical Parish or District of R. Michael

The undermentioned Houses are situate within the Boundaries of the

Cols. 1	2	3	4	5	6	7	8	9	10	11	12	13	14	15	16
No. of Schedule	ROAD, STREET, &c., and No. or NAME of HOUSE	HOUSES In-habit-ed	Un-in-habited (U.) or Building (B.)	Number of rooms occupied if less than five	NAME and Surname of each Person	RELATION to Head of Family	CON-DITION as to Marriage	AGE last Birthday of Males	Females	PROFESSION or OCCUPATION	Employer	Employed	Neither Employer nor Employed	WHERE BORN	If (1) Deaf-and-Dumb (2) Blind (3) Lunatic, Imbecile or Idiot
4	7, Charlotte Street ("Queen's Arms")	1			Michael Morrison	Head	M	31		Licensed Victualler	X			London; Islington	
					Mary J. Do.	Wife	M		30					Salop; Condover	
					Ellen Do.	Daur.			7 mo.					Do. Shrewsbury	
					Elizabeth Morrison	Mother	Wid.	59		Living on her own means				Do. do.	
					Ann Fox	Serv.	S		28	General Servant			X	Scotland; Aberdeen	Idiot
					Catherine Doyle	Serv.	S		24	Barmaid			X	Ireland	
					Adolphe Morlier	Lodger	Wid.	45		Steam Engine Maker—Fitter			X	France	
5	8, Charlotte Street	1			André Dubois	Do.	S	33		Bridle Maker	X			Jersey; St. Helier	
					Lambert Norden	Head	M	32		Grocer (Master)		X		Cumberland; Wigton	
					Emma Do.	Wife	M		30	Relate				Do. Longtown	
					William Do.	Son		12		Do.				Salop; Ludlow	
					Henrietta Do.	Daur.			9	Do. do.				Do. do.	Deaf-and-Dumb
					George Benson	Stepson	S	19		Grocer's Shopman		X		London; Shoreditch	
					Jane Manley	Serv.	S		22	General Servant			X	Scotland	
			4		William B. Yates	Serv.	M	47		Banker's Clerk		X		Yorkshire; Leeds	
					Harriet Do.	Wife	M		42					Salop; Bridgnorth	
7	1, Third Lane	146	5		Sophia White	Serv.	S		18	General Servant			X	Staffordshire; Bilston	
					William Houghton	Head	M	72		Coal Miner		X		Do. Tamworth	
					Anne Do.	Wife	M		69					Devon; Honiton	
8	2, Third Lane	1			Thomas Rose	Head	Wid.	66		Retired Farmer			X	Cardea; Crediton	
					Henry Rose	Son	S	32		Organist		X		Do. Crediton	
					Emma Do.	Niece	S		41	Court Artist			X	London; R. Pancras	
9	Do.	1			Jane Griffiths	Boarder	S		10	Court Artist (Apprentice)			X	Salop; Pulton	
		200			Walter Campbell	Head	S	23		Ship Carpenter			X	Durham; Sunderland	

(The next Schedule to be entered on the following page.)

End of the Enumeration District of R. Michael.

| Total of Houses and of Tenements with less than Five Rooms | 4 | 4146 | 232 | | | | Total of Males and Females... | 11 | 13 | | | | | | |

Note.—Draw the pen through such of the words of the headings as are inappropriate.

iii

PG 27/490

1891 enumerator's return

iii.

EXAMPLE

Administrative County _Shropshire_

Civil Parish _of Shrewsbury, St. Chad_   Ecclesiastical Parish _of Shrewsbury, St. George_

The undermentioned Houses are situate within the Boundaries of the —
County Borough, Municipal Borough or Urban District _of Shrewsbury_ — Ward of Municipal Borough or of Urban District _of_ — Rural District _of_ — Parish or Township _of Seen Within_ — Parliamentary Borough or Division _of Shrewsbury_ — Town or Village or Hamlet _of_

Cols 1		ROAD, STREET &c. and No. or NAME of HOUSE	HOUSES				NAME and Surname of each Person	RELATION to Head of Family	Condition as to Marriage	Age last Birthday		PROFESSION OR OCCUPATION	Employer, Worker, or Own account	If Working at Home	WHERE BORN	If (1) Deaf and Dumb (2) Blind (3) Lunatic (4) Imbecile, feeble-minded
			3	Inhabited 4	Uninhabited: In occupation 5	Not in occupation / Being built 6	Number of rooms occupied if less than five 7	8	9	10	Males 11	Females 12	13	14	15	16	17
4	7, Cheddle Street	1				John Smith	Head	M	58		Glass Merchant	Employer		Surrey; Godstone	
						Sarah Do.	Wife	M		49				Scotland	
						Thomas Do.	Son	S	28		Clergyman (Church of England)			Surrey; Godstone	
						Robert Do.	Son	S	25		Solicitor's Clerk			London; Paddington	
						Jean Aubel	Visitor	S	50		House Agent	Own account		France (French subject)	
						Ellen Roberts	Serv.	S		22	Housemaid—Domestic			Canada	
						Jane Edwards	Serv.	S		25	Cook—Domestic			Kent; Bexley	
5	4, Hard Lane (Knackilow Farm)	1				George Wood	Head	Wid.	52		Farmer	Employer		Hants; Basingstoke	
						Ann Do.	Son	S	28		Farmer's Son	State		Cambridge; Newmarket	
						Flora Do.	Dau.	S			Living on own Means			do.	Blind from Childhood
						Flora Do.	Aunt	S		74				Ireland	
						Richard Webb	Serv.	S	24		Carter on Farm	Worker		Sussex; Chichester	
6	2, Bird Lane	1				Martha Jones	Serv.	S		20	General Servant—Domestic			Hants; Basingstoke	
	3, Do.	1				John Cox	Head	M	40		Machine Minder (Cotton Mill)	Worker		Lancs; Oldham	
						Elizabeth Do.	Wife	M		40				Do. do.	
						William Do.	Son	S	22		Weaver Worsted	Worker		Yorks; Bradford	
						Sophia Do.	Dau.	S		18	Cotton Spinner	Worker		Do. do.	
						Margaret Hall	M-in-law	Wid.		74	Retired Laundress	Worker	At home	Caernarvon; Conway	
						Mary Cox	Gr.d.	S		12	Scholar		At home	Lancs; Oldham	
						James Smith	Boarder	S	26		Coffee Miner	Worker		Germany (British subject)	
7		1				Walter Johnson	Head	Wid.	30		Railway Engine Stoker	Worker		Northampton; Oundle	
						James Do.	Son		10 mo.					Isle of Man	
8	4, Do.	1				Edward Martin	Head	Wid.	55		Shoemaker	Own account	At home	London; Newington	
	5, Do.	1				Hannah Do.	Dau.	S		22	Dressmaker	do.	do.	Do. do.	
						Julia Do.	Dau.	S		19	Shirtmaker	Worker	do.	Do. do.	Imbecile
											End of the Enumeration			Parish of Shrewsbury, St. George	

The next Schedule to be entered on the following page

| | Total of Schedules of Houses and of Tenements with less than Five Rooms | 5 | 4 | 1 | | 2 | 2 | Total of Males and of Females... | | | 13 | 12 | | | |

NOTE.—Draw your pen through each words of the headings as are inapplicable.

1901 enumerator's return

Appendix 4 Geographical and administrative areas in the census

Administrative county: *see* **County**

Ancient county: *see* **County**

Borough
There is agreement neither on what constituted a borough in the Middle Ages, nor how many there were. Some towns had ancient charters, others claimed the right by prescription, some were incorporated, and some had several claims to the title. Among the distinguishing marks of a borough were the possession of its own offices and institutions which included some degree of exemption from the county's jurisdiction, special schemes of taxation, the right to hold fairs and markets, and the right to representation in Parliament.

The 1832 Reform Act took away the right to parliamentary representation from some boroughs, extended the parliamentary limits of others, and created boroughs with parliamentary status. This destroyed the identity between municipal and parliamentary boroughs. The Municipal Corporations Act of 1835 officially established boroughs with municipal powers, either by inclusion in the schedule to the Act or by later charter. Towns of exceptional importance were made county boroughs, either by inclusion in the original schedule in the 1888 Local Government Act or by later charter. This status carried complete exemption from the jurisdiction of the surrounding or adjacent administrative county. Some important boroughs returned more than one MP to Parliament.

Chapelry
A territorial division of a parish. The ancient parish can be seen as the area served by a parish church. With the rise of population additional churches were built within the parish, and parts of the latter came to be assigned by custom to these secondary churches under the name of chapelries.

City
An important urban settlement with the rank and title 'city' conferred by royal authority. The term is commonly associated with cathedral towns but there is no necessary correlation. Birmingham, for example, became a city in the nineteenth century but did not have a cathedral.

Civil parish: *see* **Parish**

County
The ancient counties, sometimes called the geographical counties, are geographical entities whose origins lay in the period before the Norman Conquest in 1066. They were either Anglo-Saxon kingdoms whose size made them suitable

administrative units when England was unified in the tenth century, or artificial creations formed from larger kingdoms.

The counties of England were able to send two knights of the shire to represent them in Parliament. As a result of the 1832 Reform Act and subsequent legislation the areas which formed the basis of parliamentary representation (the parliamentary counties) were redrawn and were no longer coterminus with the ancient counties.

The 1834 Poor Law Amendment Act grouped parishes together into poor law unions for the purpose of poor law administration. These often included parishes in two or more ancient counties. These unions were the basic building blocks of the registration districts. The registrar general created an artificial poor law or registration county for census purposes, by grouping under one county those unions predominantly comprised of parishes within the ancient county. The registration counties and the ancient counties do not, therefore, necessarily coincide.

A new system of administrative counties was established by the 1888 Local Government Act. These counties were made up of municipal boroughs, and urban and rural sanitary districts. They sometimes coincided with the existing ancient counties but when an urban sanitary district extended into two counties, the whole of the district was accepted as within that county which contained the largest portion of the population of the district according to the census of 1881. Certain ancient counties were subdivided. The three ridings of Yorkshire, for example, each became administrative counties.

County borough: *see* **Borough**

Ecclesiastical parish: *see* **Parish**

Extra-parochial places
Certain geographic areas were not organised as parishes and hence were called extra-parochial. There were a number of reasons for this arrangement, including association with the crown (Windsor Castle), with a religious house before the Dissolution, or with a cathedral chapter, or with other corporate bodies such as inns of court. These areas enjoyed virtual exemption from taxation; from maintaining the poor, since there was no overseer; from the militia laws because there was no constable to make returns; and from repairing the highways because there was no official surveyor.

In 1857 the privileges of those areas were curtailed by an Act 'to provide for the relief of the poor in extra-parochial places'. This decreed that places named extra-parochial in the *1851 census report* were to be deemed parishes for this purpose and to have overseers of the poor appointed. In the case of very small areas, the place was annexed to an adjoining parish, if the consent of the owners and occupiers of two-thirds (in value) of the land was obtained. In the case of places not specified as extra-parochial in the *Census report* the Act was merely permissive, and therefore, largely inoperative. An Act of 1868 declared that every extra-parochial place existing on 25 December 1868, should be added to the next adjoining civil parish with which it had the longest common boundary. Some lighthouses and small islands, which were not contiguous with any parish, were overlooked in the Act and remained extra-parochial. There were still many places extra-parochial from ecclesiastical parishes which enjoyed special privileges under church law or custom.

Hamlet
Subdivision of a parish; a settlement smaller than a village.

Hundred
Subdivision of ancient counties which can already be found in Domesday Book. It was supposed to have originally comprised land capable of supporting 100 families. By the late nineteenth century it had lost all administrative importance.

Improvement commissioners district: From 1748 onwards ad hoc authorities known as improvement commissioners were set up by local acts of Parliament in urban areas to deal with the paving, lighting and cleansing of streets. Some of these authorities were given police powers. They consisted of owners of freehold property above a specified value, or of persons elected by the local rate-payers, with an ex-officio element, e.g. local justices of the peace. Improvement commissioners were abolished by the 1894 Local Government Act.

Lathe
An ancient division of the county of Kent, containing several hundreds or liberties. Each lathe had a lathe-reeve or under-sheriff.

Liberty
A district analogous to an extra-parochial place, only of a larger extent, in which the normal course of law as it affected the hundred did not apply.

Local board district
The 1848 Public Health Act provided for the establishment of a local board of health, elected by the ratepayers, in every urban area where the inhabitants requested it, or where there was a high death-rate. The boards were abolished by the 1894 Local Government Act.

Metropolis
The City of London enjoyed independence as a county of itself from early times. As the population spilled out beyond the City's original limits of about a square mile, there was no single government unit to exercise authority over the enlarged area. The 1855 Metropolis Management Act created a Metropolitan Board of Works to undertake sanitary works for an area which by then included parts of Middlesex, Surrey and Kent, without altering jurisdictions in any other matters.

The area of the Metropolis (with minor boundary changes) became a separate county in 1889 when the general system of administrative counties was established. As a result of the 1899 London Government Act the London Administrative County was subdivided into metropolitan boroughs.

Municipal borough: *see* **Borough**

Municipal ward: *see* **Ward**

New parish: *see* **Parish**

Parish
It is very difficult to define the term 'parish'. Originally the parish was more a collection of rights than a specific area. Before the seventeenth century the parish existed for ecclesiastical purposes, as the area under the jurisdiction of a clergyman with the cure of souls. With the establishment of the Elizabethan poor law in 1597, the parish began to acquire secular functions, in this case the relief of the poor. Parishes which existed before 1597 and which thereafter had secular as well as ecclesiastical functions were called 'ancient parishes'.

'Civil parishes' were administrative units which only had secular functions, and were commonly defined as areas for which a separate poor rate could be assessed. The existence, alteration or abolition of these units had no effect on the ecclesiastical arrangements of the locality. Many civil parishes were areas at first subordinate to a mother church which had come in time to enjoy independence, such as hamlets, tithings, townships, chapelries and liberties. If a separate poor law rate was levied in the subordinate unit, it could be called a 'hamlet', 'township', and so on, and/or a 'parish'. In order to avoid confusion the 1866 Poor Law Amendment Act required that these areas should be called 'parishes'. Many extra-parochial places had already become civil parishes in 1857.

From 1597 onwards 'ecclesiastical parishes' were established for purely ecclesiastical purposes. They were more numerous than civil parishes, especially when efforts were made to build new churches in urban areas where the population was increasing. Many ecclesiastically subordinate areas within parishes, such as chapelries, were raised to parochial rank, and many formed which had no previous status. In the nineteenth and twentieth centuries a number of statutory provisions allowed the creation of many different types of ecclesiastical or 'new' parishes. It was not unusual for a parish to be refounded to gain privileges and rights conferred by newer statutes.

Parliamentary borough: *see* **Borough**

Parliamentary borough division
The 1885 Redistribution of Seats Act created single-member constituencies, and it was necessary to divide up multiple-member boroughs.

Parliamentary county: *see* **County**

Parliamentary county division
From 1832 onwards a number of statutes divided the counties established for parliamentary purposes, e.g. East and West Kent.

Poor law union
Under 'Gilbert's Act' of 1782 certain parishes were, with the consent of their inhabitants, combined into unions for poor law purposes. This partial reorganisation was made more general in England and Wales by the 1834 Poor Law Amendment Act, which vested the management of poor relief in boards of guardians whose sphere of responsibility extended to all the parishes which made up their union. In forming these unions consideration was given to local convenience and the preservation of existing parishes, rather than to administrative consistency. Many unions were thus partly in two or more ancient counties.

Rape
A division of the county of Sussex, containing several hundreds or liberties. The term may have been derived from 'hrepp' or rope, the Norman method of dividing the land.

Registration county: *see* **County**

Registration district
When civil registration was established in England and Wales by the 1836 Births and Deaths Registration Act, the poor law union areas were generally adopted as registration districts. A superintendent registrar of births, deaths and marriages was appointed for each.

Registration division

For the purpose of statistical investigation in England and Wales registration districts thought to possess common characteristics were grouped into registration divisions. Before 1851 there were twenty-seven such areas which were usually made up of counties or groups of counties. In some cases, however, the pre-1851 divisions included parts of counties. Division IX, for example, comprised Norfolk and the northern part of Suffolk. The pre-1851 divisions were not used for census purposes. In 1851 (with the exception of the area around London) whole registration counties were grouped into eleven divisions, these being:

I   LONDON, comprising the portions of Middlesex, Surrey and Kent within the limits of the registrar general's bills of mortality.

II   SOUTH-EASTERN DIVISION, comprising Surrey and Kent (outside the London division), Sussex, Hampshire and Berkshire.

III   SOUTH-MIDLAND DIVISION, comprising Middlesex (outside the London division), Hertfordshire, Buckinghamshire, Oxfordshire, Northamptonshire, Bedfordshire and Cambridgeshire.

IV   EASTERN DIVISION, comprising Essex, Suffolk and Norfolk.

V   SOUTH-WESTERN DIVISION, comprising Wiltshire, Dorsetshire, Devonshire, Cornwall and Somersetshire.

VI   WEST-MIDLAND DIVISION, comprising Gloucestershire, Herefordshire, Shropshire, Staffordshire, Worcestershire and Warwickshire.

VII   NORTH-MIDLAND DIVISION, comprising Leicestershire, Rutland, Lincolnshire, Nottinghamshire and Derbyshire.

VIII   NORTH-WESTERN DIVISION, comprising Cheshire and Lancashire.

IX   YORK DIVISION, consisting of Yorkshire.

X   NORTHERN DIVISION, comprising Durham, Northumberland, Cumberland and Westmorland.

XI   WELSH DIVISION, comprising Monmouthshire, South Wales and North Wales.

Registration sub-district

Registration districts were divided into sub-districts consisting of combined parishes or localities in which resident registrars were appointed for the registration of births, marriages and deaths.

Rural district: *see* **Sanitary district**

Rural sanitary district: *see* **Sanitary district**

Sanitary district

The Public Health Acts of 1874 and 1875 created new authorities with responsibilities in public health. Urban areas, already included in municipal boroughs or other bodies such as towns with improvement commissioners, were to form urban sanitary districts, the numbers of which were gradually enlarged in succeeding years. The rest of the country was divided into rural sanitary districts which were coterminus with poor law unions less the areas in urban sanitary districts. The system was abolished by the 1894 Local Government Act, which transformed urban and rural sanitary districts into general-purpose urban districts and rural districts within the framework of administrative counties.

Tithing
Subdivision of a parish, generally for poor law purposes.

Town
A settlement more regularly built than a village and having more complete and independent local government. This term could be applied to cities and boroughs having special privileges and titles but also to smaller settlements which might be indistinguishable from villages except, perhaps, that they had the right to hold periodical markets or fairs.

'Town (not being a city or borough)': *see* **Town**

Township
Subdivision of a parish, generally for poor law purposes.

Urban district: *see* **Sanitary district**

Urban sanitary district: *see* **Sanitary district**

Village
Subdivision of a parish, generally for poor law purposes; a centre of habitation in a country district.

Wapentake
Rather than being made up of hundreds, some northern and eastern counties settled by Danish invaders prior to 1066 were divided into wapentakes. The term was perhaps derived from an Old Norse word meaning a waving or brandishing of weapons as a means of signifying consent to a decision taken by the assembled inhabitants.

Ward
Subdivision of a parliamentary constituency for electoral purposes.

Ward of urban district: *see* **Ward**

Appendix 5   Geographical data sought on each page of the enumerators' books

Each page of the enumerators' returns had spaces or boxes at the top for information on the administrative units covered therein. Some of these units were, of course, mutually exclusive, and the enumerators were expected to strike out those which did not apply.

1841

1   City or borough
2   Parish or township

1851

1   Parish or township
2   Ecclesiastical district
3   City or borough
4   Town
5   Village

1861

1   Parish [or township]
2   City or municipal borough
3   Municipal ward
4   Parliamentary borough
5   Town [not being a city or borough]
6   Hamlet, tything, etc.
7   Ecclesiastical district

1871

1   Civil parish [or township]
2   City or municipal borough
3   Municipal ward
4   Parliamentary borough
5   Town [not being a city or borough]
6   Village or hamlet, etc.

7   Local board [or improvement commissioners district]
8   Ecclesiastical district

1881

1   Civil parish [or township]
2   City or municipal borough
3   Municipal ward
4   Parliamentary borough
5   Town or village or hamlet
6   Urban sanitary district
7   Rural sanitary district
8   Ecclesiastical parish or district

1891

1   Administrative county
2   Civil parish
3   Municipal borough
4   Municipal ward
5   Urban sanitary district
6   Town or village or hamlet
7   Rural sanitary district
8   Parliamentary borough or division
9   Ecclesiastical parish or district

1901

1   Administrative county
2   Civil parish
3   Ecclesiastical parish
4   County borough, municipal borough or urban district
5   Ward of municipal borough or of urban district
6   Rural district
7   Parliamentary borough or division
8   Town or village or hamlet

Appendix 6   Summary tables in the enumerators' books

1841

1   Number of males and females in vessels on inland navigable waters, in mines or pits, in barns or sheds, in tents or in the open air, or not enumerated as inmates of any dwelling house.
2   The probable number of males and females temporarily present or temporarily absent from the district, and the cause thereof.
3   Number of persons emigrated to the colonies or foreign countries since 31 December 1840.

1851

1   Number of separate occupiers, houses (inhabited, uninhabited, being built), males and females recorded on each page of the nominal returns.
2   As in first table but for each named parish or township. Persons to be divided into those in and out of houses.
3   Estimated number of males and females in vessels on inland navigable waters, in barns or sheds, in tents and in the open air.
4   Number of males and females temporarily present.
5   Number of males and females temporarily absent.

1861

1   Number of males and females temporarily absent, and the reasons for their absence.

2   Number of males and females temporarily present, and the reasons for their presence.
3   Number of schedules, houses (inhabited, uninhabited, being built), males and females in each named parish or township, or parts thereof. Persons to be divided into those in and out of houses.
4   Number of above on each page of the nominal returns.

1871

1   Number of males and females temporarily absent, and the reasons for their absence.
2   Number of males and females temporarily present, and the reasons for their presence.
3   Number of schedules, houses (inhabited, uninhabited, being built), males and females in each named civil parish or township, or parts thereof.
4   Number of the household schedules filled in by the enumerator.
5   Number of elements in 3. on each page of the nominal returns.

1881

1   Number of males and females temporarily absent, and the reasons for their absence.
2   Number of males and females temporarily present, and the reasons for their presence.
3   Number of schedules, houses (inhabited, uninhabited, being built),

males and females in each named civil parish or township, or parts thereof.

4 As above for other administrative areas.

5 Number of elements in 3. on each page of the nominal returns.

1891

1 Number of schedules, houses (inhabited, uninhabited, being built), tenements of less than five rooms, and males and females in each named civil parish or township, or parts thereof.

2 As above for other administrative areas.

3 As above but for each page of the nominal returns.

1901

1 Number of schedules, houses (inhabited, uninhabited, being built), tenements of less than five rooms, and males and females in each named civil parish or township, or parts thereof.

2 As above for other administrative areas.

3 As above but for each page of the nominal returns.

Bibliography

Manuscript sources

1831 Census, Clergyman's Returns (Public Record Office [hereafter PRO]: HO 71).

1841 and 1851 Census Returns (PRO: HO 107).

1861 Census Returns (PRO: RG 9).

1871 Census Returns (PRO: RG 10).

1881 Census Returns (PRO: RG 11).

Acreage Returns (PRO: HO 67).

Census Returns (Guildhall Library: MS various).

Census Returns: Correspondence and Papers (PRO: RG 19).

Crosby Ravensworth Parish Records (Cumbria Record Office, Kendal: WPR/7).

Forms and Instructions for taking the Census (PRO: RG 27).

General Register Office Letter Books (PRO: RG 29).

Home Office: Domestic Correspondence, George IV and later (PRO: HO 44).

Home Office: Registered Files (PRO: HO 45).

John Sutherland's diary and 1861 census book (in the possession of Mrs Doris Jackson of Birk Nott, Heversham, Cumbria).

London School Board Statistical Committee (Greater London Record Office: SBL 908).

Public Record Office, General Correspondence (PRO: PRO 1).

Public Record Office: Inspecting Officer's Committee: Correspondence and Papers (PRO: PRO 17).

Receivers' Accounts of Land and Assessed Taxes: Subsidiary Documents (PRO: E 182).

Reference Maps of Registrars' Districts (PRO: RG 18).

Treasury Board Papers (PRO: T 1).

Parliamentary papers

1812 census report: abstract of the answers and returns, PP 1812 XI [316 & 317].

Minutes of evidence taken (session 1830) before the select committee on the Population Bill, PP 1840 XV [396].

1841 census report: abstract of the answers and returns, PP 1844 XXVII [587].

1851 census report: tables of the population and houses, PP 1851 XLIII [1399].

1851 census report: population tables, I, PP 1852–53 LXXXV [1631].

1851 census report: population tables, II, PP 1852–53 LXXXVIII Pt 1 [1691–I].

1861 census report, PP 1863 LIII Pt 1 [3221].

Return relating to elementary education (civil parishes), PP 1871 LV [201].

1871 census report, PP 1873 LXXI Pt II [872–I].

1881 census report, PP 1883 LXXX [c.3797].

1890 report of the Treasury Committee on the Census, PP 1890 LVIII [c.6071].

1891 preliminary census report, PP 1890 XCIV [c.6422].

1891 census report, PP 1893–94 CVI [c.7222].

Explanatory letter of the registrar general of England and Wales relative to the census of 1891, PP 1894 LXIX [331].

1901 census report, PP 1904 CVIII [Cd.2174].

Evidence and index to the second report of the Royal Commission on Public Records, Vol II, Pt III, PP 1914 XLVI [Cd.7456].

Articles, books and unpublished papers

M Anderson, *Family structure in nineteenth century Lancashire* (London, 1971).

M Anderson, 'Standard tabulation procedures for the census enumerators' books 1851–1891', in *Nineteenth-century society*, ed. E A Wrigley (Cambridge, 1972), pp 134–145.

M Anderson, 'The study of family structure', in *Nineteenth-century society*, ed. E A Wrigley (Cambridge, 1972), pp 47–81.

A Armstrong, *Stability and change in an English country town. A social study of York 1801–51* (London, 1974).

W A Armstrong, 'Social structure from the early census returns', in *An introduction to English historical demography*, ed. E A Wrigley (London, 1966), pp 209–237.

W A Armstrong, 'The use of information about occupation. Part 2. An industrial classification, 1841–1891', in *Nineteenth-century society*, ed. E A Wrigley (Cambridge, 1972), pp 226–310.

W A Armstrong, 'The census enumerators' books: a commentary', in *The census and social structure*, ed. R Lawton (London, 1978), pp 28–81.

G Belfiore, 'Compulsion and community in the Essex textile districts', unpublished paper in the author's possession.

A A Benjamin, 'Human afflictions: a study of the north Ceredigion census returns, 1851–1871', *Ceredigion*, X (1985), pp 155–160.

C Booth, 'Occupations of the people of the United Kingdom, 1801–81', *Journal of the Statistical Society of London*, XLIX (1886), pp 314–444.

M Bouquet, *Family, servants and visitors: the farm household in nineteenth and twentieth century Devon* (Norwich, 1985).

B R Bristow, 'Population and housing in nineteenth-century urban Lancashire: a framework for investigation', *Local Population Studies*, XXXIV (1985), pp 12–26.

V C Burton, 'A floating population: vessel enumeration returns in censuses, 1851–1921', *Local Population Studies*, XXXVIII (1987), pp 36–43.

W Cobbett, *Rural rides* (Harmondsworth, 1983).

B I Coleman, 'The incidence of education in mid-century', in *Nineteenth-century society*, ed. E A Wrigley (Cambridge, 1972), pp 397–410.

M Conk, 'Labor statistics in the American and English census: making some invidious comparisons', *Journal of Social History*, XVI (1982–83), pp 83–102.

M J Cullen, *The statistical movement in early Victorian Britain: the foundations of empirical social research* (Hassocks, 1975).

A Davin, 'Working or helping? London working-class children in the domestic economy', in *Households and the world economy*, eds. J Smith, I Wallerstein, H Evers (London, 1984), pp 215–232.

P Deane and W A Cole, *British economic growth, 1688–1959* (Cambridge, 1969).

Dictionary of National Biography (London, 1896).

M Drake, 'The census, 1801–1891', in *Nineteenth-century society*, ed. E A Wrigley (Cambridge, 1972), pp 7–46.

H J Dyos, *Victorian suburb. A study of the growth of Camberwell* (Leicester, 1977).

Eighth report of the deputy keeper of the public records (London, 1847).

Eighth annual report of the keeper of the public records (London, 1967).

Eleventh annual report of the keeper of the public records (London, 1970).

Encyclopaedia Britannica (London, 1969).

J M Eyler, *Victorian social medicine: the ideas and methods of William Farr* (London, 1979).

C H Feinstein, *National income, expenditure and output of the United Kingdom, 1855–1965* (Cambridge, 1972).

Fifteenth report of the deputy keeper of the public records (London, 1854).

J Foster, *Class struggle and the Industrial Revolution: early industrial capitalism in three English towns* (London, 1974).

Fourth annual report of the keeper of the public records (London, 1963).

J Gibson, *Census returns on microfilm, 1841–1881. A directory to local holdings* (Plymouth, 1982).

D V Glass, *Numbering the people: the eighteenth century population controversy and the development of census and vital statistics in Britain* (London, 1978).

D V Glass & P A M Taylor, *Population and emigration: government and society in nineteenth century Britain* (Dublin, 1976).

J A S Green, 'A survey of domestic service', *Lincolnshire History and Archaeology*, XVII (1982), pp 65–69.

D Grigg, 'Farm size in England and Wales, from early Victorian times to the present', *Agricultural History Review*, XXXV (1987), pp 179–189.

E Higgs, 'The tabulation of occupations in the nineteenth-century census, with special reference to domestic servants', *Local Population Studies*, XXVIII (1982), pp 58–66.

E Higgs, 'Domestic servants and households in Victorian England', *Social History*, VIII (1983), pp 203–210.

E Higgs, 'Domestic service and household production', in *Unequal opportunities: women's employment in England 1800–1918*, ed. A V John (Oxford, 1986), pp 124–150.

E Higgs, *Domestic servants and households in Rochdale, 1851–1871* (New York, 1986).

E Higgs, 'Women, occupations and work in the nineteenth century censuses', *History Workshop Journal*, XXIII (1987), pp 59–80.

E Higgs, 'The census as a medical survey, 1841–1911', a paper read on 27 November 1987 before the Wellcome Symposium on the History of Medicine entitled 'The General Register Office in the Nineteenth Century: a Comparative Perspective'.

E Higgs, 'The struggle for the occupational census, 1841–1911', in *Government and expertise: specialists, administrators and professionals, 1860–1914*, ed. R M MacLeod (Cambridge, 1988), pp 73–86.

P Horn, 'Child workers in the Victorian countryside: the case of Northamptonshire', *Northamptonshire Past and Present*, VII (1985–86), pp 173–185.

J Knodel, 'An exercise on household composition for use in courses in historical demography', *Local Population studies*, XXIII (1979), pp 10–23.

P Laslett & R Wall, *The household and family in past time* (London, 1974).

R S Holmes, 'Identifying nineteenth-century properties', AREA, VI (1974), pp 273–276.

The census and social structure: an interpretative guide to nineteenth century censuses for England and Wales, ed. R Lawton (London, 1978).

R Lawton, 'Census data for urban areas', in *The census and social structure*, ed. R Lawton (London, 1978), pp 82–145.

P Laxton, 'Liverpool in 1801: a manuscript return for the first national census of population', *Transactions of the Historical Society of Lancashire and Cheshire*, CXXX (1980), pp 73–113.

P McHugh, *Prostitution and Victorian social reform* (London, 1980).

T MacKay, *A history of the English poor law* (London, 1904), III.

B R Mitchell, *Abstract of British historical statistics* (Cambridge, 1962).

M Nissel, *People count: a history of the General Register Office* (London, 1987).

Office of Population Censuses and Surveys & General Register Office, Edinburgh, *Guide to census reports, Great Britain 1801–1966* (London, 1977).

Parish registers (London, 1845).

W T R Pryce, 'The census as a major source for the study of Flintshire society in the nineteenth century', *The Journal of the Flintshire Historical Society*, XXVI (1973–74), pp 114–143.

P E Razzell, 'The evaluation of baptism as a form of birth registration through cross-matching census and parish register data: a study in methodology', *Population Studies*, XXVI (1972), pp 121–146.

E Roberts, *Women's work 1840–1940* (London, 1988).

P Rushton, 'Anomalies as evidence in nineteenth-century censuses', *Local Historian*, XIII (1978–79), pp 481–487.

Seventh report of the deputy keeper of the public records (London, 1846).

J A Sheppard, 'The east Yorkshire agricultural labour force in the mid-nineteenth century', *Agricultural History Review*, IX (1961), pp 43–54.

Sixteenth annual report of the keeper of the public records (London, 1975).

K D M Snell, 'Agricultural seasonal employment, the standard of living, and women's work in the south and east, 1690–1860', *Economic History Review*, 2nd Series, XXXIV (1981), pp 407–437.

Thirteenth report of the deputy keeper of the public records (London, 1852).

Thirteenth annual report of the keeper of the public records (London, 1972).

C Thomas, 'Rural society in nineteenth-century Wales: south Cardiganshire in 1851', *Ceredigion*, VI (1970), pp 388–414.

S Thomas, 'The enumerators' returns as a source for a period picture of the parish of Llansantffraid, 1841–1851', *Ceredigion*, IV (1963), pp 408–421.

S Thomas, 'The agricultural labour force in some south-west Carmarthenshire parishes in the mid-nineteenth century', *Welsh History Review*, III (1966–67), pp 63–73.

D Thomson, 'Age reporting by the elderly in the nineteenth century census', *Local Population Studies*, XXV (1980), pp 13–25.

P M Tillott, 'Sources of inaccuracy in the 1851 and 1861 censuses', in *Nineteenth-century society*, ed. E A Wrigley (Cambridge, 1972), pp 82–133.

Twenty-fourth report of the deputy keeper of the public records (London, 1863).

F Whitehead, 'The GRO use of social surveys', *Population Trends*, XLVIII (1987), pp 45–54.

Nineteenth-century society, ed. E A Wrigley (Cambridge, 1972).

E A Wrigley, 'Baptism coverage in early nineteenth-century England: the Colyton area', *Population Studies*, XXIX (1975), pp 299–316.

E A Wrigley & R S Schofield, *The population history of England 1541–1871* (London, 1981).

E A Wrigley, 'Men on the land and men in the countryside: employment in agriculture in early-nineteenth-century England', in *The world we have gained. Histories of population and social structure*, eds. L Bonfield, R M Smith and K Wrightson (Oxford, 1986), pp 295–336.

Index